Shroud

Robert K. Wilcox

Shroud

Macmillan Publishing Co., Inc.

New York

Collier Macmillan Publishers

London

Macmillan Publishing Co., Inc.
866 Third Avenue, New York, N.Y.   10022
Collier Macmillan Canada, Ltd.

Library of Congress Cataloging in Publication Data
Wilcox, Robert K
  Shroud.
  1. Holy Shroud. I. Title.
BT587.S4W5   232.9′66   77-4960
ISBN 0-02-628510-X

First Printing 1977

Designed by Jack Meserole

Printed in the United States of America

Photo Credits

GA	Geoffrey Ashe	GR	Msgr. Giulio Ricci
LC	Leonard Cheshire	LV	Leo Vala
HSG	Holy Shroud Guild, Esopus, New York	RKW	Robert K. Wilcox
KJ	Kendall Johnson	DW	David Willis
HN	Hans Naber	EW	Ernest Wood

To Bego,
my parents, and
her parents

Acknowledgments

In addition to all of those mentioned in the book who gave of their time and resources, I would like to give special thanks to: Frs. Rinaldi and Otterbein, for their continual support throughout the preparation of this manuscript; Marge Keasler, for her editorial help prior to my sending the manuscript to the publisher; and William Griffin, my editor at Macmillan, for his vision and revision resulting in the final draft.

Contents

Preface

IS THE SHROUD OF TURIN—the linen cloth reputed to be the garment in which Jesus was buried—a medieval forgery, an occult phenomenon, a proof of Jesus' resurrection?

To answer this question, I traveled halfway around the world to interview sindonologists, sindonophiles, and just plain shroud quacks, and to consult specialists in the half-dozen sciences touching upon the shroud. (*Sindon,* by the way, is the Greek word for "shroud.")

During these encounters I have met "the man with the shroud bus" in London and "the guy with the shroud show" in Southern California; the German black marketeer who had a seven-day technicolor vision of Jesus' suffering and death on the wall of his bedroom; the American priest who suspended himself from a cross more than seven hundred times in order to learn the mechanics of crucifixion; the British fashion photographer who developed three-dimensional-looking film portraits of the face in the shroud; the Italian monsignor who has fashioned a grisly crucifix based on the superrealistic data on the shroud; physicists of all kinds (optical, nuclear, radiation) and one Nobel Prize-winning organic and nuclear chemist; pathologists from several countries who have conducted macabre but shroud-related experiments on the newly and unclaimed dead; people at the Eastman Kodak Company in Rochester, the FBI in Washington, and the Hiroshima Peace Memorial Museum; a fingerprint expert in Minnesota; one disappointed film producer; and one disappointed king —Umberto II, exiled from Italy in 1946—who owns the shroud.

It is a weird story, a wild story, and one that is filled with not a little wonder. Jeane Dixon says the shroud will prove to be the most important occult phenomenon of the 1970s. Pope Paul VI calls it Christianity's most important relic. What you call it will depend on how you approach the evidence. Approach it with a closed mind, and you will follow in the shameful steps of the English Jesuit and the French abbé who, at the turn of the century, claimed the shroud was a painted forgery; yet neither had ever examined the shroud, and both refused to accept the testimony of those who had examined it and said that there was no paint on the fabric. Then there was the British Museum curator in the 1950s who refused to consider historical evidence that the shroud existed before the fourteenth century, but under another name. Finally, there was the *Scientific American* editor in the 1970s who refused to accept the fact, amply supported by correspondence, that in the 1930s an editor from that magazine had, after weighing the evidence, come to accept the shroud's authenticity.

Approach the shroud with an open mind. Ask all the appropriate, necessary, difficult questions—questions such as the following:

Is the imprinted cloth unique?

Could the linen of the cloth and the herringbone twill have been manufactured and distributed throughout the Mediterranean world two thousand years ago?

Are the imprints on the cloth those of a human corpse?

Do the suffering, death, and burial details recorded on the shroud correspond to the sufferings and death described in the Gospels?

If the work is a forgery—a possibility that should be seriously and thoroughly entertained—how would the forger have accomplished his or her act?

What is the statistical probability that the anonymous victim suffered, died, and was buried in exactly the same way as Jesus?

Was the man in the shroud the man we call Jesus Christ?

Did the man in the shroud, did Jesus, come back to life again?

How, in fact, was the image imprinted on the cloth of the shroud?

Before you accept or reject the shroud, meet the people I've interviewed; weigh the evidence encountered in books, journals, and magazines; examine the photographs of the shroud; consider the icons and the mandylions; contemplate the contemporary reconstructions of the man in the shroud—then, and only then, will you be able to decide for yourself whether the shroud of Turin is a medieval forgery, an occult phenomenon, or a proof of the resurrection of Jesus Christ.

Shroud

Miami

"THEY'RE going to show the shroud after all these years? You've got to be kidding!"

I didn't mean to be rude, especially when the other party was calling me long distance, but it was 1973 and the last time the shroud had been put on public display was in 1933; before that, in 1931; and before that, in 1898.

"I've just returned from Turin. There really is going to be a public exposition, this time on television. . . ."

The voice on the other end of the line was shaky, not only because Fr. Peter Rinaldi had recently had a throat operation and was learning to speak again, but also because he could hardly contain himself with enthusiasm.

"And the cardinal has assured me that all experts invited to Turin for the occasion will see the shroud in person."

Rinaldi, who was an interpreter for non-Italian-speaking visitors to the 1933 exposition, is one of America's leading sindonologists. Now a Salesian priest in Port Chester, New York, he had been prodding the Turin authorities for the previous nine years to show the shroud in public again. His hope, along with that of the other sindonologists around the world, was that such an exposition would lead to a full-scale scientific investigation, which, in turn, would lead to a final vindication of the shroud as the linen cloth put around the body of Jesus after it was taken down from the cross.

"When is it going to take place?" I asked.

"In about three months' time—around Thanksgiving."

"Can you get me a pass to attend as one of the experts?"

I wasn't really an expert, but I had been writing about the shroud for more than two years. My interest in it had been aroused by a wire story I'd read about a German who believed that Christ had not died on the cross. What impressed me about the story was not so much the arguments deduced from the shroud, but the fact that something else besides the New Testament existed as proof that Jesus Christ really did exist. I made a quick trip to Turin, visited the Center for Sindonology there,

1

interviewed as many sindonologists as I could find in that city and in Rome, then returned home to Miami to write four articles on the shroud. They appeared first on the front pages of the Miami *News* and later in syndication through the North American Newspaper Alliance.

"That shouldn't be a problem," said the priest. "Just send me a letter saying you'll be covering the event for your newspaper."

The shroud was made of ivory-colored, almost yellow linen, and was disfigured in several distinct ways. Wrinkles zig-zagged the 14½-foot length and 3½-foot width of the cloth whenever it was hung for exposition. Burn marks from a fire in 1532 ran down the cloth's sides. Water marks resembling rough-cut diamonds, made when the sixteenth-century fire was doused, could be seen with the naked eye.

Also appearing on the shroud were two softly diffused but distinct impressions of a body. They were difficult to see up close, but at a distance they stood out in subtle brown. It was as though the cloth had been wrapped around a body —not in mummy fashion, but lengthwise—beginning at the heels and proceeding up the back to the base of the skull, then over the head and down the face to the toes.

The face was owl-like, almost grotesque. The eyes were open and staring, with what looked like pinholes for pupils. The nose was long and thin—a line in the center of the face. The mouth was a smudge beneath the nostrils. The hair appeared coarse and stringy, and hung almost to the neck in what appeared to be two braids. Between the hair and the sides of the face there was a curious space.

The feet appeared to be missing from the frontal image, and the legs were little more than lines tapering from the trunk. But the thighs, knees, and calves could be discerned, and the hands were folded over the loins in repose. The stomach, chest, and arms were easily recognizable on the frontal image, whereas the head, shoulders, and buttocks stood out on the dorsal.

The dull red stain of blood was everywhere. Large droplets from under the hairline suggested the entrance points of

Giulio Clovio, a sixteenth-century artist, rendered the shroud both before and after the body of Jesus was wrapped in it. (HSG)

thornlike instruments. Small lacerations all over the body could easily have been the result of indiscriminate and interminable flogging. Wounds from nails resulted in large seepages on the hands as well as thin trickles on the arms. The gash in the side showed the most bleeding; blood had gathered around the hole, then flowed down the sides of the body and across the small of the back.

These were the images Secondo Pia expected to see as he peered into the tray of chemicals and waited for the negative plate to develop. The year was 1898, and he had been commissioned to make the first photographs ever of the shroud. But what he saw as he held the dripping plate up to the red light was something far different. The face was alive with expression; its details were almost portraitlike. The eyes were closed and tranquil as though the figure were asleep. The mouth was full, with mustache above and beard below. The nose was long and prominent, with gradations of shadow down the sides. The hair, strands of which were matted with blood, appeared soft and smooth.

What Pia was looking at were *positive* images, and what he saw on the cloth itself, the photographer concluded, must be *negative* images. Exactly how these images had been transferred to the shroud he could not say. What was clear was that Jesus had left not only his "photograph" on the shroud but also a visual record of what happened to him in the bloody hours before his death. ■

En route to Europe

Before leaving Miami, I had stuffed my briefcase full of all the clippings, articles, and books about the shroud that I had on file. There would be many moments to fill during my trip, and if I wanted to write again about the shroud, this time in depth, I would have to master every detail about its history and every theory about its origins.

The first thing I picked out of my case was a batch of clippings having to do with world reaction to the Pia photographs.

"The photography was stupendously successful," said Turin's

Corriere Nazionale. "It represents an exceptional value to history, science, and religion."

"The rumor of the marvelous event spread like wildfire in Turin," said a correspondent for the London *Daily Telegraph.*

"The picture makes an indelible impression," said Genoa's *Cittadino.*

"A miraculous event," proclaimed *Osservatore Romano,* and the article from the Vatican's newspaper of record was reprinted around the world.

Not all the world, however, was favorably impressed.

"It would be interesting to see some of Monsieur Pia's other negatives," said a French photographic journal, "to determine if the phenomenon observed on the one plate also reproduced itself on the others. If it hadn't, then one can only conclude that it was the case of either an accident or an optical illusion."

Refutation of this and similar charges, I was yet to learn, would come years later. At least three other people had photographed the shroud in 1898, and each had had the same results as Pia.

It was May 3, 1931, the first of a twenty-one-day exposition during which two million people would pass by the shroud in St. John's Cathedral in Turin.

When the great doors were shut at 10:30 P.M., Giuseppe Enrie walked down the center aisle toward the main altar. Enrie, editor of *Vita Photographica Italiana* and owner of a photo studio and laboratory in Turin, had two hours in which to photograph the shroud.

The shroud was hanging in a gilded frame over the main altar, and the first step in the photographing process was to take it down from its perch. Maurilio Cardinal Fossati, archbishop of Turin, directed the move, and several prelates mounted the tiered altar and unscrewed the bolts that held the fifteen-foot-long frame in place. Slowly, carefully, they handed the frame to priests waiting below, who then placed it at the foot of the altar. This took about fifteen minutes.

Noticing that creases in the cloth, especially around the top of the head and the lower chin, marred the image, Fossati unfastened the cloth from the frame, smoothed it out, and

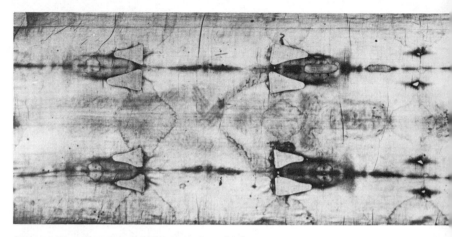

Above   The shroud as it appears to the naked eye.
Below   As it appears on the film negative. These technically perfect
photographs were taken by Giuseppe Enrie during the 1931 exposition (HSG)

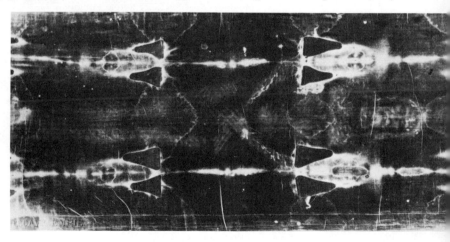

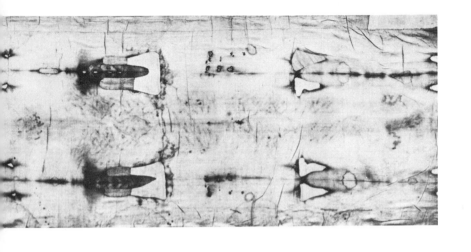

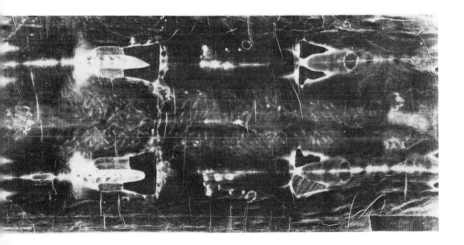

refastened it. The creases were still visible. Fr. Antonio Tonelli, an expert in the textile aspects of the shroud, tried his hand at smoothing the creases; he too had no success. By now, fifteen more minutes had passed, and Enrie, who had already set up the lights and camera, was getting impatient. With a shrug, Fossati motioned to the photographer to begin.

Enrie focused first on the burn patches; they were the easiest marks to see. He checked the image in the viewfinder with a magnifying glass. Then he opened the shutter for a time exposure. When nine minutes had passed, he closed the shutter, took the photographic plate out of the camera, and rushed toward the sacristy where he had set up a makeshift darkroom.

With the help of Secondo Pia, now seventy-six years old, and two others, he set about developing the plate. One hundred sixty seconds passed before Pia shouted, "It's the same!" There in the tray of chemicals was the face he knew so well —only this time the image was clearer and sharper. Enrie took the plate out of the developer and held it up to the light. There was no question about it—the revelation had been repeated! They hurried back into the sanctuary to show the plate to the cardinal and his staff.

By 12:30 A.M. Enrie exposed six more plates, each focused on the shroud as a whole. He and his friends spent the rest of the night developing the plates, and by 10:00 A.M. he was ready to submit the resulting prints to the cardinal for his inspection. Six days later the prints were stamped "Authorized for reproduction," and copies were sent to a number of publications around the world.

On May 19, Enrie took three more photographs of the shroud, which was still on display in its glass-covered frame; each shot was of one-third of the cloth; the result was a composite of the whole shroud, and these too were officially approved.

On the evening of May 22, he took three close-ups of the shroud without its glass covering: one of the face, one of the back and shoulders, and, with a lens that would magnify seven times, one of the wound on the wrist.

To avoid the same kind of charges of fraud that had plagued Pia after his 1898 photographs had been distributed around the world, Enrie invited five professional photographers to study his plates. They verified that none had been retouched and that all had accurately captured what the naked eye could see on the surface of the shroud. They signed a document swearing to these conclusions.

From that time on, Pia's photographs were retired, and the Enrie photographs became the official pictures of the shroud given out by ecclesiastical authorities in Turin. The charges of hanky-panky in the darkroom have never been brought up again. ■

Lisbon

UMBERTO OF SAVOY, who was crown prince in 1931 and is now king of Italy, lives in exile in Portugal, near Lisbon. Since he and his family have owned the shroud for centuries, it was logical to assume that he would most certainly know more about it than anyone else. As I drove from the airport in Lisbon north along the road to Cascais—Father Rinaldi had arranged the interview —I hoped the king would be able to tell me who actually controls the shroud today.

In fifty miles' time I reached the small, picturesque fishing village, with its masted boats bobbing all around the circumference of the blue bay. Crossing a bridge at the northern tip of the bay, I found the king's villa overlooking the Atlantic. "Villa Italia" read the inscription on the stone wall. The iron gates were open, and I drove up a short, pebbled driveway to a large, two-story stone house. A servant opened the heavy wooden doors and ushered me into a drawing room, the first room to the left off a short, high-ceilinged entrance hall. In a moment the king's secretary appeared, and after conferring with someone behind him hidden from my view, escorted me inside.

The king lifted his hand in greeting. "How is Father Rinaldi?" he asked me in English. He appeared taller than he did in pictures I'd seen of him standing beside his father, and younger than his seventy years.

Umberto II of Savoy on his estate in Portugal, 1973 (RKW)

The room was a large study lined with portraits of Savoys. Papers lay strewn over a massive desk. The king was in the midst of writing his memoirs, or so he said. We sat down. As I began to set up the tape recorder, he put up his hand. He was sorry but he could not allow the interview to be recorded; I'd have to take notes.

The talk began with the king describing scenes of the various expositions he'd attended and knew something about.

Prior to the 1868 exposition, he said, Princess Clotilde (1843–1911) got down on her knees and mended the deteriorated backing of the shroud. This was an indication of how revered the shroud was among his family members.

At the time of the 1933 exposition, a *New York Times* report had said there was an old belief within the royal house that as long as the shroud remained in the possession of the Savoys, the house would never fall; yet the house had fallen after a 1946 plebiscite in which the Italian people expressed their preference for a republic instead of the monarchy. I mentioned this story to the king; he said he was not familiar with the belief.

The shroud was shown only on important occasions, mostly family ones. The 1898 exposition had been held in honor of his father's, Victor Emmanuel III's, wedding; and of course the 1931 exposition had commemorated his own wedding. The 1933 exposition had been held in honor of the nineteen-hundredth anniversary of Christ's death and resurrection. To show the shroud more often, he said, would make it a commonplace.

"Who controls the shroud?" I asked.

"Before I left Turin," the king replied, "the family always made decisions concerning the shroud—after consultation with the pope, of course. During World War II, my father ordered that the shroud be taken to southern Italy because of the possibility that it might be damaged by bombs. When the war ended, I personally ordered it back to Turin. But when I left Italy, I told the archbishop of Turin that he would be in charge. 'I won't be here,' I said, 'so you will know best what to do.' That is the way it has remained. He makes the final decisions."

The king said he would favor scientific tests on the shroud, but the initiative would have to come from Turin. There was a security problem right now, he went on; twice in recent months attempts had been made to steal the shroud from the chapel in which it resides. No one had been caught, and the chapel is now rigged with an elaborate alarm system.

Half an hour had passed, and voices could be heard in the drawing room. "I am sorry," the king's secretary said, "but others are waiting." The king rose, I thanked him, and as I left the room, four well-dressed men entered, kissed the king's hand, and said that they wished he still were king.

As I pulled out of the driveway and headed back to the Lisbon airport, the king was on the front steps of his villa posing for pictures.

One day in 1932 Dr. Pierre Barbet was shown Enrie's life-size photographs of the shroud; a friend of his had been to the 1931 exposition and wanted his opinion of the anatomy of the shroud figure. Looking at the photographs, Barbet was impressed with the realism of the images. Using the bloodstains as his guide, he decided to test whether the man in the shroud had actually been crucified. The only way to conduct such a test, of course, would be to crucify someone himself. And this is precisely what he did.

As head surgeon at St. Joseph's Hospital, Paris, he had access to unclaimed bodies, and twenty-four hours after death he could experiment on cadavers.

On the floor was a cross: the upright, about seven feet in length; the crossbar intersecting it about one foot from the top of the upright. Onto the cross he rolled the corpse and stretched its arms out at right angles. Poising a square nail— the sort of nail the Romans used—not at the palm, but at the wrist, he drove it through the flesh and into the wood with one blow; then he nailed the other hand. He next drove a nail through the middle of the left foot; then, pressing the sole of the right foot flush against the wood, he drove the same nail through the flesh and into the cross.

Raising the cross from the floor, Barbet knew that his theories would literally either stand or fall when he brought the cross to a totally upright position and slid the beam into a hole on the platform. When he did so, the body slumped

14

down about ten inches. The chest area expanded in size as though the victim had taken a deep breath and were about to exhale. The head was pulled forward and down, the chin touching the collarbone. The knees jutted out. The body stayed on the cross.

At some later date Barbet formulated these and other observations into a physiological sketch of the crucifixion and gave them to Charles Villandre. A doctor himself, and also a sculptor, Villandre incorporated all the shroud data into a crucifix with corpus that was starkly realistic for its time. ■

Turin

SNOW was on the Alps when I arrived, and after I had warmed up, I decided to go to the archdiocesan office. I wanted to interview Fossati's successor, Michele Cardinal Pellegrino, and to pick up whatever material about the shroud that the office had prepared for foreign journalists who no doubt would be covering the event.

What I noticed initially upon entering the building was the lack of activity. The first showing of the shroud in forty years was surely a historic occasion, and I had expected it to generate high, if subdued, excitement. I later found out that once the archdiocese had decided to announce the exposition, it had launched what it felt was an elaborate campaign to publicize the event: special commissions were appointed, proclamations issued, newspaper articles written, Eucharists celebrated, and a security firm hired. But that was a month ago. Now, a few days before the event, none of this material was available in the Turin chancery.

Suddenly I was confronted with a problem. I didn't speak Italian; no one in the chancery spoke English; and what little printed matter I could pick up was not in English.

When I returned later with an interpreter from the hotel, I got little more information. There would be a press conference on Friday in preparation for the exposition on Saturday. I might be able to get an interview with the cardinal later in the week. Only the cardinal and his spokesman, Msgr. José Cottino, knew the details, and they were not available for interview right now.

My interpreter was an elderly woman who was accustomed to

dealing with tourists. As a go-between to extract information, she was less than adequate, for when given vague replies, or no answer at all, she did not press for more. I decided to return to my hotel, the Ambasciatori, where I could read more of the books and articles I had been accumulating on the shroud.

In 1939 a sindonological congress was held in Turin. One of the topics under discussion was the burial of Jesus. Was he buried hastily, or was his body given a full ritual interment? If the body had not been washed, then the images on the shroud could have been formed by vapors rising from the sweat. But if the body had been not only washed, but also packed with spices, then the images on the shroud could have been formed by direct contact.

Prior to the congress, two Italian pathologists had conducted experiments by spreading aloes, myrrh, turpentine, olive oil, and sometimes animal blood on the faces of corpses available to them. They then applied linen cloths to the contours of the faces in an attempt to lift off an image as sharp as the shroud's.

"Prof. Romanese of the Royal University of Turin and Prof. Judica-Cordiglia of the Royal University of Milan have presented extraordinary results," wrote Turin's newspaper *L'Italia*. "They have made imprints that even have the diffusion of the shroud, without, of course, surpassing its beauty or perfection. This encourages the possibility of some day being able to make imprints exactly like the shroud's."

When the official record of the 1939 proceedings was published in 1941, it referred to Romanese and Judica-Cordiglia as pioneers. In reality, however, the contact images they produced fell far short of the realism exhibited by the shroud itself. ■

Msgr. José Cottino came quickly into the small room adjoining the shroud chapel where I and my new translator, a more able woman than the first, were waiting early Tuesday morning. Cottino announced with half a smile that he didn't have much time and asked me to be brief.

16

I decided to skip the preliminaries and get right to the main point.

"What were the findings of the secret commission appointed in 1969 to investigate the shroud?"

"There have been no results beyond what was announced in early 1970," said the priest. "We have told you that many times. The commission members were only to see what condition the relic was in. And the only thing that could be determined on the spot was that the man in charge of deciding if the Carbon 14 test could be used decided that it could not be."

"Why?"

"Carbon 14 would damage the shroud," said Cottino. "The test involves burning a piece of the material, and too large a piece would have to be destroyed. And there is no assurance that the test would be accurate. Carbon 14 can only give you a date accurate within two hundred years, plus or minus. And the cloth had been handled so much, and been in and out of at least two fires, that its carbon content might very well have been affected under such adverse conditions. Carbon 14 is good for objects that have been protected in the earth or in caves, but not for the shroud."

"Are you sure nothing else resulted from the commission members' examining the shroud for three days?"

"Yes, I'm sure. There was nothing else," said Cottino. "But you must understand I can only answer your religious questions pertaining to the shroud. The cardinal is the only one who can tell you anything about the commission."

"But aren't you one of the officers of the commission?"

"Please, I can tell you nothing more about the commission. If you have something to ask me about the exposition, perhaps I can help."

"How about the names of the commission members?"

Cottino's half smile was replaced by a look of irritation. "We feel that the commission members will be better able to complete their work if they are not known," he said. "We do not want a great debate going on while they are working."

My translator was becoming embarrassed by the heat of the exchange. I decided to change the subject to the exposition.

Here Cottino opened up a bit. He explained that the idea behind this upcoming exposition was to increase devotion to the shroud by showing it to as many people as possible. By putting it on Italian television, the exposition would reach millions of Italians, and the authorities would be able to gauge their devotional as well as political reactions. "The shroud was always a symbol of the monarchy," Cottino said, "especially right after the war."

When I asked a question about the history of the shroud, Cottino referred me to Fr. Piero Coero-Borga, author of *The Holy Shroud of Turin,* which was published in 1961 by the Confraternity of the Shroud in Turin, and secretary of the Center of Sindonology, the shroud museum in the city.

> Evasively was also the way Cardinal Fossati had answered the Nazis' repeated request, during World War II, to see the shroud. Although they said they wanted to view it for scholarly and devotional purposes, the cardinal had already spirited the shroud from its resting place over the altar in the shroud chapel to a stone fortress overlooking Avellino, 140 miles south of Rome. Built in the twelfth century and accessible only by a dirt road, the building now was the Benedictine monastery of Monte Vergine. When the shroud arrived, it was placed in a wooden box, sealed, and placed under the main altar in the chapel. If the monastery were bombed, the monks could rush it to a cave in the heart of the mountain.
>
> In 1946, in gratitude for their preserving the shroud while war raged up and down the country, Cardinal Fossati gave the monks and several invited guests a private showing of the shroud. ■

When Fr. Piero Coero-Borga greeted me at the door of the shroud museum, he was unpretentious, almost businesslike. Like Cottino, he didn't have much time to discuss the shroud; he was heavily involved, he said, in preparations for the exposition. But he did take the time to show me and my interpreter around the museum, which was one building of several surrounding a small, paved square that was open to the sky. It wasn't very big—nothing more than a large room really—with items from the shroud's past on shelves and tables. Secondo Pia's camera was the biggest display piece; it stood in one corner, like a finely carpentered, natural-grained doghouse on stilts. Positioned carefully on a table in the center of the room were books of clippings going back to 1900. A gallery of shroud personalities—mostly Italian —glowered from the walls.

When the tour was over, the three of us walked across the courtyard to Coero's office. Letters from shroud enthusiasts all over the world were stacked on his desk, and as curator of the museum and custodian of all official shroud information, he would answer them all. After we sat down, I brought up the secret commission again.

"I would like to tell you who they are," Coero replied, "but we are all sworn to secrecy. If, however, you read the newspapers, you may learn something."

From a desk drawer he pulled out a handful of clippings, handed them to me, and then turned to his voluminous correspondence. While he was thus engaged, I went through the clippings with my translator. I checked for outright admissions, for facts that only commission members would know, for details about the photographing of the shroud that had not been released by the archdiocese. With the aid of these and other sources I was able to piece together a list of probable commission members; some of the names I would eventually verify; others would remain simply good guesses.

"The commission found nothing new, you know," said Coero, looking up from his correspondence. "For them everything has already been decided. They are living in the past. They think the 1930s were the glory years and nothing new can be found. For me, it is impossible to think that anyone could examine the shroud in 1969 and not find something new."

"The archdiocese," he added, "was going to let some of the scientists of the commission take out a small part of the shroud with blood on it. But the scientists could not get together on how to examine it. When the authorities saw the disagreement, they decided such a liberty would not be wise."

It was noon. I thanked Coero and, with my interpreter, headed for the door. But before we reached it, he advised me to check the

guest list at the Ambasciatori. Perhaps some of the commission members would be coming to Turin for the exposition.

As I left, I felt that the shroud was doomed to be forever enveloped in official secrecy. Perhaps I could get a few rays of light from the cardinal, with whom I had an appointment in the afternoon.

On May 1, 1950, the first international shroud congress was convened in the Majestic Pontifical Chancellery Palace near the Vatican, Rome. The Turin *cultores,* hosts of the congress, had invited scholars from all over the world to come to the eternal city and to start anew what had almost been lost in the holocaust.

Representing the United States was Fr. Edward Wuenschel; he was the one who had translated, edited, and indeed sold the shroud article by Paul Vignon to *Scientific American* in 1937. In a paper entitled "The Holy Shroud and the Burial of Christ," he told the congress that the shroud was not in conflict with either the known methods of Jewish burial or the New Testament Scriptures.

Representing France was Dr. Pierre Barbet, who delivered a paper, "Proof of the Authenticity of the Shroud in the Deposits of Blood," which he based on the realism exhibited by the mysterious blood images.

Also from France was Msgr. Joseph R. deMelin, vicar general of the diocese of Troyes, where in the fourteenth century Geoffrey deCharnay, the church officials at Lirey, and Pierre d'Arcis had been embroiled with the shroud.

There were four delegates from Italy:

Giovanni Judica-Cordiglia, the pathologist from the University of Milan, delivered two papers—one on the new studies of the origin of the imprints; the other on anthropological observations.

Fr. Pietro Scotti, professor of chemistry at the University of Genoa, gave a general overview of scientific research since 1898.

Msgr. Pietro Savio, a Vatican archivist, detailed his extensive research into the Church's libraries for documents that might shed light on the misty history of the shroud.

22

Lorenzo Ferri, a professor at the University of Rome and a sculptor who had made a marble statue modeled on the figure in the shroud, shared his anatomical observations with the congress.

From Spain had come Dr. Tomas L. Luna of the University of Saragossa. He presented a brief history of Spain's devotion to the relic: in 1454, it seems, the kingdom of Aragon had been granted a license to collect money for the shroud; a convent in Toledo had a painting of the shroud on one of its walls; a church in Madrid had a copy of the shroud that was said to have been pressed against the shroud of Turin on May 3, 1620.

The sole German present was Dr. Hermann Moedder, a radiologist from Cologne. He reported on experiments in which he had student volunteers hang from crosses in simulated crucifixion. Unlike Barbet, he believed that death was caused by the pooling of blood in the body's lower parts.

Several papers were received and read *in absentia*.

R. W. Hynek, the doctor who had conducted studies on the death of Christ, was to have come from Czechoslovakia to speak on the physical agonies of the crucifixion. The Communist government, however, had refused to give him a visa.

Dr. Muitz Eskenazi did not come from Istanbul, Turkey, but his paper attacking the authenticity of the shroud was read into the record of the congress. He offered no new evidence for his position, and the arguments he used had already been refuted many times over by the European and American sindonologists.

The four-day congress ended with solemn devotions in Turin, and although nothing really new came out of it, the press saw fit to give the proceedings full coverage. ∎

The cardinal's office was large and cold; the walls were built of gray stone blocks. Velvet drapes flanked the windows, dark portraits hung on the walls, and the chairs my interpreter and I sat on were upholstered in leather. On the coffee table was a copy of Rinaldi's book *It Is the Lord* which, I discovered on opening it, was personally inscribed by the author. We sat down on the lumpy leather chairs and waited and whispered.

"How big was Jesus Christ?" asked *Time* magazine in its May 15, 1950 issue. "Was he a strongly built man, 5 feet 10 inches tall, with long, delicate hands and feet, a right shoulder slightly lower than the left? Did he have a brain weighing approximately 1,492 grams?"

The American news magazine was reporting on the first International Congress of Studies of the Holy Shroud which had met two weeks before in the huge frescoed hall of the Papal Chancellery in Rome.

Lorenzo Ferri, the professor and sculptor from the University of Rome, believed that Jesus was taller than previously reported. The shroud showed him to have been six feet one or two inches tall and to have had the lithe limbs of an artist. When laid in the tomb, the body was hunched up in the shape of an **S**, with knees bent upward and back and with neck curling over. Therefore, when and if stretched flat, the body would be longer than the imprints on the shroud show.

Ferri was backed up in this belief by Dr. Luigi Gedda, a Rome anatomist, who said the man in the shroud was at least six feet tall. The proof he offered was measurements he had taken when the shroud was shown to the Benedictines at Monte Vergine in 1946.

Gedda also pointed out that the man in the shroud had an appreciable slump in his right shoulder and concluded that Jesus must have been a right-handed carpenter.

The *Time* story ended with an equal list of pros and cons on the authenticity of the shroud. ∎

Nearly an hour had passed since the time the interview with Michele Cardinal Pellegrino was supposed to have begun, when a pale-faced young man in a cassock entered the room. He motioned for us to follow him. Beyond the curtains through which he led us were a succession of rooms, and in the last of these was the cardinal. He was sitting at a desk with another curtain behind it. I put out my hand; he put out his; and we shook limply.

Before I could ask my first question, he said he wanted it

Dr. Hermann Moedder (right), a radiologist at St. Francis Hospital, Cologne, conducting an experiment in crucifixion (HSG)

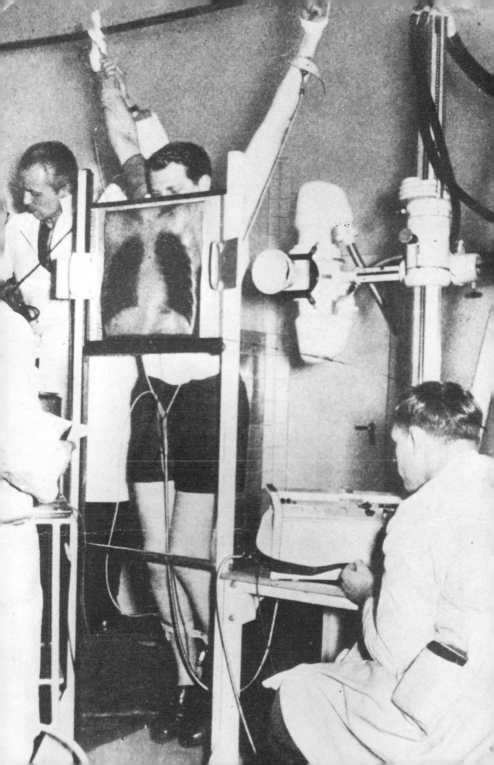

understood that "all authority and answering power" had been transferred to Monsignor Cottino.

I acknowledged his statement, but before I could ask my second question, he said that a press conference would be held the next day during the course of which all questions pertaining to the shroud exposition on television Saturday night would be answered.

I said I knew that, and was just about to ask him for a comment on the international interest in the shroud, when he said that the holy relic had inspired much devotion among the faithful.

There was nothing left to say, it seemed, but to thank him and leave.

In the cab heading back to the Ambasciatori, I concluded that the twentieth century was not a good one for public relations in Turin.

In reporting on the first International Congress of Studies of the Holy Shroud in May 1950, the secular press focused on the how-did-Christ-die debate. The physicians at the congress had been split between asphyxiation and the pooling of blood in the body's lower parts.

The religious press, however, zeroed in on the issue of authenticity.

The first story filed by Fr. Max Jordan, who was covering the congress for the National Catholic News Service, dealt with the German scholars. Although not present at the meetings, they had attacked the authenticity of the shroud on scriptural grounds. Jordan's final dispatch at the end of the congress reported that evidence for and against authenticity was about even.

Somewhat later, the London *Tablet* ran a story to the effect that the impression made just by the photographs of the shroud was a very deep one. "The first thought likely to occur is: 'But how very strongly the figure resembles the Christ of any number of old masters!' "

The article concluded with a double negative: "No one who believes in the genuineness of the Holy Shroud can be accused of undue credulity."

26

When a ten-year-old victim of osteomyelitis heard of the shroud in 1955—a bus carrying shroud photographs and other sindonalia was touring England—she asked her parents if she could see the real thing. Perhaps it could cure her twisted leg, stop her internal hemorrhaging, and dry the running abscesses on her skin. "I'm suffering like Jesus, aren't I?" she asked her mother. "If I am blessed with the relic, I know I'll get well."

The girl's name was Josephine Wollam, and she got in touch with the gentleman who was touring England in the shroud bus. He went to visit Josie and decided to try to make the girl's wish come true. He didn't know how he would be able to get in to see the shroud, but perhaps Josie would succeed where scholars and sindonologists had failed. Almost before travel arrangements could be made—the tickets were delivered to them on the railroad platform—he and Josie set off first for Cascais, Portugal, to get King Umberto's blessing on the undertaking.

By the time they arrived in Turin, the press had got wind of the mercy mission. They were met at the train by reporters, photographers, priests, and several representatives of the king; Umberto had already telephoned his approval of the mission. Apparently the king's influence was nil, for when the entourage arrived the following morning at the cardinal's residence, Fossati was not inclined to see them. However, when he heard that Josie had brought with her a white dress made especially for the occasion by her mother, he telephoned the Vatican for permission.

It was 4:15 when they entered the cathedral through the side door and went up the steps of the Chapel of the Holy Shroud. The doors were bolted and locked behind them. Only the cardinal, some priests, the guardian of the shroud, two nuns, and the king's representatives were present with Josie and her sponsor; the press had been allowed to deceive themselves into thinking that the private exposition would take place that night.

When Josie returned from the sacristy where she had gone

to change her dress, the cardinal beckoned her to his side. He was kneeling in front of the shroud altar. A moment of silence and prayer followed; then the cardinal gave a signal. Two priests approached the altar, climbed up the steps to the vault over the altar, and unlocked the three devices on the safe door. They reached inside and brought out a long, slender, embroidered casket, and with the help of two more priests, they carried it down and deposited it on a table next to the cardinal.

Another moment of silence, another prayer, then the casket was placed in Josie's lap. When nothing of a miraculous nature seemed to happen, the casket was put back on the table. Josie looked up at the cardinal as if to ask if she could see and touch the shroud itself.

The cardinal huddled with the priests around him. Then he examined the seals surrounding the casket and even tried to pry open the lid without breaking the seals. When unsuccessful, he sent for a pair of scissors, cut the silk tapes, and opened the lid.

The two priests reached inside and brought out the shroud, which was encompassed in red silk affixed with yet another set of seals. Gently, they placed the shroud against her twisted leg, and there began a profound silence throughout the chapel. When nothing happened, Josie looked at the cardinal again. He told her she could put her hand inside the silk covering, but there was nothing else he could allow her to do.

As the shroud was replaced in the casket and the casket restored to its vaulted shrine, Josie and her patron prayed. On leaving, she told the cardinal she felt better, and the cardinal reportedly looked pleased.

No miraculous cure had ever been attributed to the shroud of Turin. Nothing unusual occurred during Josie's first visit, nor during another one a year later. But how can one explain the fact that as Josie grew older, her health improved? Today she is a married woman with a family of her own, and shows no signs of her former illness. ■

The shroud's resting place: a silver casket behind iron grillwork over an altar in St. John's Cathedral, Turin (HSG)

The press conference for the Friday exposition was to be held in one of the large conference rooms of the Royal Palace. Once the former residence of the Savoys, the building had been converted into a museum with some rooms used as city and church offices. The palace was attached to St. John's Cathedral; it also surrounded a courtyard, which was the size of a football field, in which the lavish processions of previous shroud exhibitions had taken place.

The conference was supposed to begin at 11:00 A.M., but by noon nothing had happened. Seventy-five local and foreign newsmen were supposed to be in the room, plus a number of shroud experts from around the world; but far fewer than that seemed to be in attendance.

While waiting, I struck up a conversation with a young woman. Pretty and blond, she was from *Newsweek*'s Rome bureau. She too had learned of the exposition through Rinaldi, and had interviewed a shroud expert in Rome before coming to Turin. And she spoke Italian.

"How big was Jesus?" asked *Newsweek* in the lead paragraph of a story in its April 29, 1968 issue. "Pious pictures of Jesus as a tall man are not accurate. Or so claims an Italian scholar who estimates that he was a shade under 5 feet 4 inches and probably weighed about 155 pounds—a normal stature for a Palestinian of Christ's era."

The article featured Msgr. Giulio Ricci, archivist at the Vatican's Congregation for Bishops and student of the shroud for many years. Ricci had made minute calculations from the shroud photos, two huge blowups of which were permanent fixtures on the walls of his spacious Rome apartment.

Ricci's first book, *The Man in the Shroud,* had been published in the 1950s. Now his later studies had interested the Vatican so much, said the *Newsweek* article, that it had published a long story on them in *L'Osservatore Della Domenica.*

Ricci based his calculations on anatomical measurements of the limbs in the shroud images. For instance, the forearms were almost 14 inches long, he said, and such a length corresponds to a 5-foot, 3-inch body. Previous calculations as

Msgr. Giulio Ricci, Vatican archivist and ardent sindonologist, making calculations on blowups of the shroud photographs (GR)

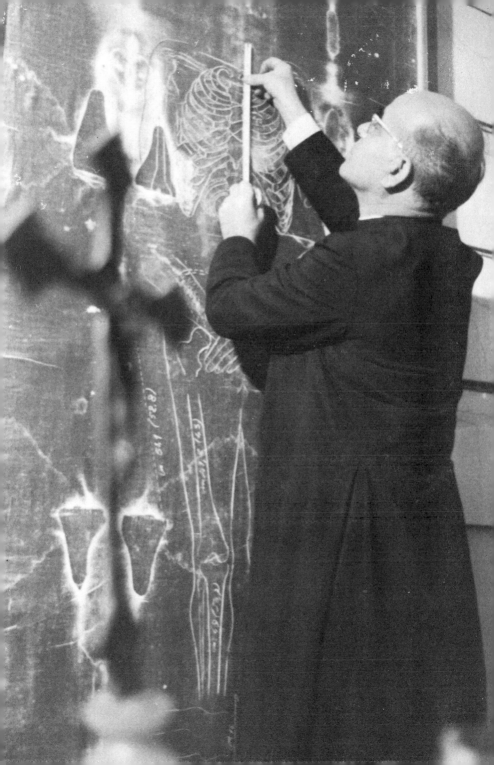

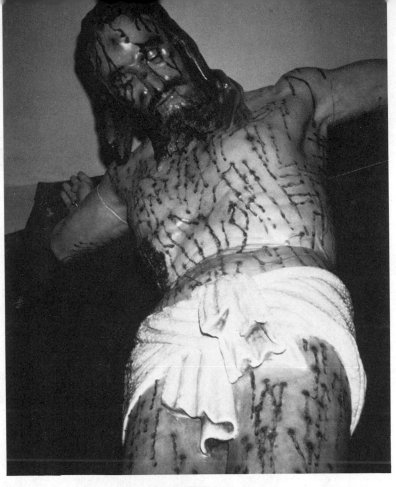

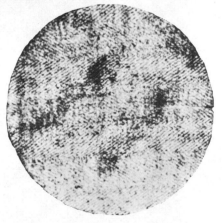

The scourging

According to Msgr. Ricci, the figure in the shroud was beaten with a Roman *flagrum*, two models of which are shown below. When laid on human skin with force, it would produce wounds that in turn would produce marks exactly corresponding to those on the shroud (opposite page, top and bottom).

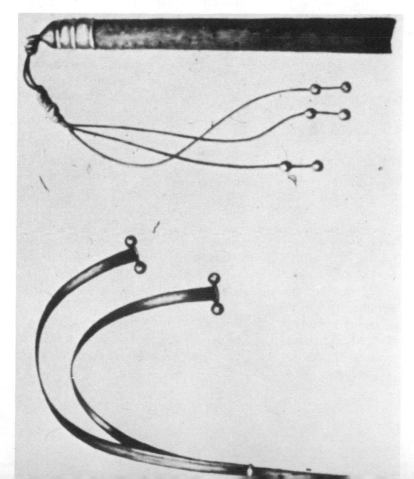

to the height of Christ were erroneous, Ricci claimed, because they were based on measurements taken from the top of the head to the tip of the toes. The toes were extended when Christ had been placed in the shroud, and therefore, according to him, measurements from or to them would make Jesus seem taller. Accurate measurements could only be made, he said, by measuring the heel.

"Together with Dr. Nicolo Miani, professor of anatomy at Rome's Sacred Heart Medical School," continued the *Newsweek* story, "Ricci spent months wrapping corpses in winding sheets to check his calculations." He also deduced that Jesus, when whipped, had been bent over in a position similar to a man in the middle of a toe-touching exercise—probably because he had had his hands tied to a "low pillar." There were at least 98 lashes to be counted on the shroud body and perhaps as many as 120, the article quoted Ricci as saying.

The *Catholic Herald,* leading Catholic weekly in England, used the *L'Osservatore* article as the basis for a feature on Ricci at approximately the same time. And shortly thereafter *Paris-Match,* one of France's largest picture magazines, also carried a story on him, which included paintings Ricci had done on the passion of Christ as deduced from the details on the shroud. ■

At 1:00 P.M. the authorities came into the room. Giovanni Judica-Cordiglia, the Milan pathologist, came in first; that he was one of the few shroud experts still around from the 1930s made him a celebrity. A small thin man with skin stretched tightly across his face and a large set of teeth, he smiled as he moved to the back of the room. A few minutes later Monsignor Cottino and Cardinal Pellegrino arrived and went directly to the rostrum, where Cottino seated Pellegrino at a table with a microphone.

"The shroud," the cardinal began, "is a moving document of the passion of Christ."

I hadn't brought a translator; I'd been told one would be provided. My heart sank as I heard the cardinal begin to speak in Italian. I listened as best I could, and Rinaldi filled me in when the conference was over.

"The imprint of the face and body of Christ on the shroud," the cardinal continued, "speak eloquently of the solemn moments of his death and resurrection. . . . The exposition is an invitation to contemplate this unique image of Christ . . . to pay attention to the running blood of his body . . . to repent, worship, and give out with grateful love. . . . Christ was crucified on account of our sins; his blood was shed for our salvation; he has saved us with his passion."

When the cardinal finished his prepared statement, Cottino said that he would answer questions from the audience.

Just how international was the commission that was formed in 1969 to conduct a secret investigation of the shroud? asked Father Rinaldi.

Not as multinational as they would have liked it to have been, Cottino answered, and they hope to add new members from other countries to the commission in the near future. "We will not be deaf to the suggestions from others."

When will the findings of this commission, which met four years ago, be released to the public?

"Be patient," said Cottino. "In a few weeks you will have all the news."

What progress had been made in fixing a date for the cloth?

Cottino rattled off the same objections to the Carbon 14 dating test that he had made to me, and then went on to add that, according to Msgr. Pietro Savio, the Vatican archivist, the three-to-one herringbone twill of the shroud had been used by weavers in at least second-century Egypt.

I asked the next question: Were the 1969 photographs taken with ultraviolet light, and if so, did they reveal any marks or symbols not visible to the naked eye?

Only color film was exposed, said Cottino, and no symbols appeared on the prints that were developed.

Would Fortunato Pasqualino, began the next question, give his impressions of the shroud?

As if on cue, Pasqualino moved from the audience to the rostrum and stood next to Cottino; he was one of Italy's leading television personalities, and he would narrate the exposition on television. A large man with heavy, purple lips and a deep, rich

The 1973 press conference

Left **Msgr. Jose Cottino**
(RKW)
Below **Michele Cardinal
Pellegrino, Archbishop of
Turin** (RKW)

voice, he said that he had never heard of the shroud before he was given the assignment to narrate the exposition. The best way of dealing with the question of the relic's authenticity, he said, was to approach it with a measure of skepticism. That way the remarkable evidence in favor of its authenticity quickly comes into focus.

Suddenly and without warning—or was it entirely prearranged? —Cottino brought the press conference to a close by saying that everyone with proper credentials could view the shroud now if they would only follow him.

Between June 16 and 18, 1969, the authorities in Turin made an extraordinary and unpublicized study of the shroud. Cardinal Fossati and his successor Cardinal Pellegrino had assembled commission of experts with a view to their examining what, if any, hurtful effects the growing industrial pollution might be having on the shroud; and to their determining with some precision if tests like the Carbon 14 dating process could be performed without detriment to the shroud. When the authorities were finally forced to admit such a study took place, they refused to name the commission members or to release their findings.

With the aid of the newspaper clippings shown to me by Father Coero-Borga in the shroud museum and as the result of a lot of hard interviewing, I would guess that there were eleven on the commission.

Three of them were clerics involved in one way or other with the shroud: Cardinal Pellegrino, Monsignor Cottino, and Msgr. Pietro Caramello, rector of St. John's Cathedral.

The eight others were scientists of one sort or another. Giovanni Judica-Cordiglia's specialty was forensic medicine, which he taught and practiced in Milan; he also took part in the 1939 and 1950 shroud congresses. Giovanni Frache taught pathology at the University of Modena; Cesare Codegone and Enzo Delorenzi were radiologists. E. Medi was a physicist from the University of Rome. Anthropologist Luigi Gedda also participated in the 1939 congress, and he took some measurements of the shroud in 1946 when it

On the next two pages, the facial image as it appears to the naked eye and as it appears on the film negative. These infrared photographs were taken by Giovanni Battista Judica-Cordiglia in 1969. (HSG)

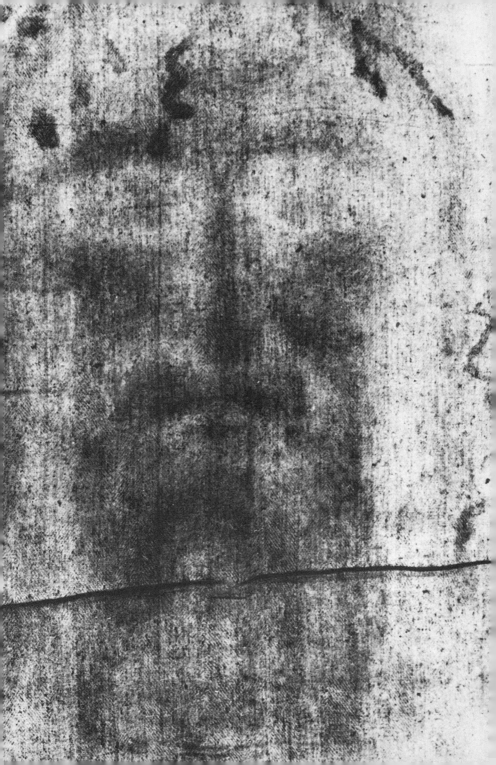

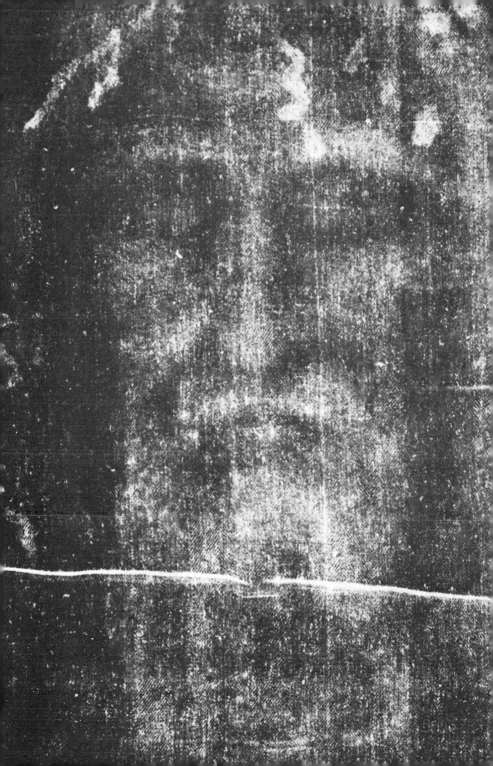

was being shown to the monks at Monte Vergine. Aurelio Ghio, a professor, and Spigo Robert, a doctor, were the ones whose names are listed as swearing to the authenticity of the color photographs taken sometime between June 16 and 18 by Judica-Cordiglia's son.

In addition to the Italians, there was a Swiss police pathologist, Max Frei; he had assisted in the investigation of Dag Hammarskjöld's death in 1961. An evangelical Protestant, Frei was the only non-Catholic on the commission.

The only noncleric and nonscientist who might have been on the commission was Lorenzi Ferri, the sculptor who was involved in the size-of-Christ debates which abounded in the early 1950s; but I was never able to verify this. ■

Follow Cottino we did—news correspondents, local press, clergy, sindonologists—down the open-air corridors bordering the huge palace courtyard, and into the palace again.

About a hundred in all, we climbed the broad marble steps curling up to the second floor, where two uniformed *carabinieri* stood in front of the Hall of the Swiss. The doors were open and through them, thirty yards away, against the far wall of the room, we could see the shroud. It was mounted vertically in a twenty-foot-high frame. We could see the man in the shroud standing in full front view; the back view was balanced, as it were, on top of his head.

At first, the group kept its distance. Then some began to inch toward the images. Afraid that the authorities might stop me from taking photographs, I hung back for a moment. I loaded my Nikon 35mm as inconspicuously as possible. An American sindonologist was doing the same thing. "I'll swap my black-and-whites for your colored shots," he whispered. I winked back, and we both started shooting.

Scaffolding had been erected against the wall facing the shroud; the television cameras would be operated from here. The pipes were already studded for the occasion with high-wattage lamps. From the scaffolding I got shots of the shroud and the crowd gesturing beneath it. Then I clambered down and, moving closer to the shroud, shot individual aspects of the images. The lower body

The shroud mounted on the wall in the Hall of the Swiss, 1973 (HSG)

on the frontal image. The large bloodstain on the wrist. The wound in the side. The face.

Since the authorities didn't seem to mind the cameras—a few others were clicking away too—I elbowed my way through the crowd to a spot about four feet in front of the relic. Suddenly it dawned on me that the glass in front of the relic wasn't reflecting any light. The television lamps illuminating the shroud were bright, even blinding, and by now I should have seen them reflected in my viewfinder. I reached out and, instead of touching glass, I felt fabric. I was touching the shroud.

How odd! Any one of the hundred-or-so people in the room could set a match to the shroud or rip it to shreds with a knife or throw a bomb at it—and no one else in the room could stop him!

However curious I was about the reason for no glass, I didn't think long on it. I put another roll of film in the camera. But just as I raised the viewfinder to my eye, an official announced that time was up; the private showing was over, and all would have to leave. I continued to shoot until a monsignor tapped me on the elbow and told me to stop. Reluctantly, I stuffed the camera back into its case and followed the group out of the hall. Next stop: to see the silver-covered wooden casket in which the shroud is kept.

The person who exploded the secrecy of the 1969 shroud commission—he said he had been tipped off by an official in Turin who wished to remain anonymous—was Kurt Berna, a German sindonologist. On June 16, the first day of the study, Berna sent leaflets and releases charging that the Church was going to alter or destroy the shroud. One reason for his concern was that the shroud proved his theory that Jesus did not die on the cross. News media in Turin and Rome picked the story up and sent it out over the global wire services. The Vatican quickly denied the charges, and the story seemed to die down.

On June 28, ten days after the secret study had been completed, Berna showed up at the Vatican gates with a briefcase full of documents and a photographer. Msgr. Charles Moeller, undersecretary of the Vatican's chief agency concerning doctrine, may have been extending the courtesy

Msgr. Charles Moeller, Vatican undersecretary, unwittingly accepting documents from German sindonologist Kurt Berna (Hans Naber) that attempted to prove Jesus was not dead when he was wrapped in the shroud (HN)

of the Vatican when he invited Berna inside the complex, but when he was photographed accepting Berna's documents, the story went round the world.

"Vatican City," United Press International (UPI) dated its story. "The President of the 'Foundation for the Holy Shroud in Switzerland' submitted documents to the Vatican which he said prove Christ was alive when he was removed from the cross. Prof. Kurt Berna said in the documents, accompanied by photographs of the shroud which reputedly was Christ's burial sheet, that marks on the shroud were caused by fresh blood. . . . This contradicts the belief of the Roman Catholic Church. It would mean that Christ recovered

43

from wounds and did not rise from death itself. There was no comment from the Vatican. . . ."

The Associated Press (AP) story had the same tone and substance. "A German author who contends Jesus Christ did not die on the cross has challenged the Vatican to reexamine the shroud believed to have wrapped Christ's body," the lead paragraph said. "Kurt Berna, author of four books on the shroud, says bloodstains on the cloth prove Christ was still alive when taken from the cross. He went to the Vatican yesterday and gave a 20-page pamphlet containing photographs and what he called documentation to the Rt. Rev. Charles Moeller. . . . The Vatican made no immediate comment."

Again the story seemed to die down, at least for five months. Then in December 1969 Berna got another tip from a source he refused to identify; a high Vatican official was reputed to have said that "the Holy Church cannot be split and teach that our Lord Jesus Christ died on the cross to free us from our sins, and at the same time worship a shroud in which no corpse ever lay. A radical solution must be found here."

Berna called the Zurich bureau of Reuter's, the English news service. The shroud was going to be destroyed, he told a Reuter's reporter, "for how else are 'radical solutions' to be understood?" Vatican officials had already tried to harm the shroud once, he added, and this time he had a quote to prove it. Reuter's, convinced of the reasonableness of his previous stories, sent this one to its subscribers around the world.

At last the Turin authorities were forced to admit what they had previously denied. On January 6, 1970, Cardinal Pellegrino released through his curia a short statement to the effect that, yes, the shroud casket had been opened; and that, no, the cloth had not been destroyed; and that experts had been asked to make suggestions how better the holy relic might be preserved for possible future studies. ■

Later, back at the hotel, I collected the impressions of the English and American sindonologists, most of whom had just seen the shroud for the first time.

Father Rinaldi, who had seen the shroud in 1933, said he was much more impressed this time. "Looking at the black-and-white photographs for so long, I had come to believe that the cloth was a maze of light and dark contrast. But in truth it is very clean-looking—like ivory—and the imprints are shadowlike. They fade . . . imperceptibly . . . into the cloth."

Everyone agreed that "imperceptively" was the appropriate word to describe the delicacy of the staining.

"Black-and-white photographs give the impression of an altogether more bloody and damaged piece of linen than is in fact the case," said one Englishman. "This arises almost entirely from the fact that pale brown takes on heightened definition and intensity when translated into black and white. You may have discovered the same effect if you have ever had old sepia photographs copied in black and white; the rejuvenation is startling."

I agreed with him. The body images were sepia, but the blood-stains were a different color.

"Carmine" or "carmine-mauve" were the terms three Englishmen used to describe the stains. "Carmine-rust" was preferred by two Americans.

And so the comments of the professional sindonologists continued.

"Were you there when they photographed my Lord?" was the title of an article in the August 1971 issue of *Esquire* magazine. In it journalist Karl E. Meyer recounted not only the ecclesiastical cover-up of the 1969 shroud commission and Kurt Berna's theory on the non-death of Jesus on the cross, but also most of the highlights in the history of the shroud since 1898. ■

Friday night was clear, and Turin was bustling with traffic as Father Rinaldi and I tried to hail a cab. We and the other sindonologists had been invited to view the exposition at the local television station. By the time we got the cab, we had been joined by Msgr. Giulio Ricci, archivist at the Vatican's Congregation for Bishops and the highest-ranking Vatican prelate with active interest in the shroud. I had first heard of Ricci in the *Newsweek* article in 1968; I met him in 1971 when I did my first story on the

shroud and had found him most cooperative. A plump, ebullient man with darting, sparkling eyes, Ricci was not at all like the secretive Catholic authorities I had had to deal with so far. In the cab he promised to help me again in any way he could.

Perhaps the most interesting deduction Ricci had made when I interviewed him in 1971 was that the man in the shroud had worn the robe first mentioned in John 19:23 and later made famous in a novel and movie. After Jesus had been scourged, said Ricci, the robe must have been flung over his shoulders. The flagellation marks that the robe or tunic would have covered—back, chest, upper arms—appear smudged on the shroud; whereas the marks that were not touched by the tunic—lower arms and legs, the face—appear decidedly more distinct. This phenomenon is especially visible, said Ricci, on the shoulders, where, all sindonologists agree, the man in the shroud carried a heavy, rough beam.

"If the cross Jesus was made to carry had been in direct contact with the lacerated shoulders, the lacerations would have been widened, forming wide sores. But, on the contrary, they have kept their shape. This would not have happened without the presence of a robe protecting the shoulders already wounded by the scourges."

Another observation Ricci made at that time was that the crown of thorns put on Jesus' head was not really a crown. "The fact that the bloodstains show that the man in the shroud wore a cap of thorns rather than a circlet is interesting, and for more reasons than have already been stated," he said. In the Western world we think of a crown as a circular band, like a wreath. But this was not true in the Orient. In the Orient, they always used a miter, a cap—a complete cap—which enclosed the entire skull, when crowning a king. And so the fact that the marks on the skull indicate a cap, rather than a wreath, was used is not only a deviation from the traditional depiction of the crown of thorns, which is evidence of authenticity. But it is also in line with what would have been done in the East, where Jesus' shroud would have come from." ■

Bust of the figure in the shroud fashioned by Msgr. Giulio Ricci (GR)

The cab deposited Ricci, Rinaldi, and me in front of the Italian national television office. Sleek and low, the building was in sharp contrast to the heavy eighteenth- and nineteenth-century structures that made up so much of Turin's skyline. Inside, plush carpeting swept down long corridors past glassed-in control rooms. Short-skirted women hurried in and out of doors. This must be Fellini's Italy, I thought, as we were met by a gray-flanneled young executive who ushered us smartly down the rest of the corridor to the wide-screened projection room.

Live, from the Hall of the Swiss, came the first exposition of the shroud in forty years. The basic scene was of the shroud mounted in its frame on the wall, with Fortunato Pasqualino on one side of it and a gallery of faithful on the other. Pasqualino narrated while the camera moved in with close-ups of the shroud or panned the invalids, children, and the aged in the gallery who appeared to be drawing some solace from the relic.

Also on the set, sitting in the middle of a line of altar boys, was Cardinal Pellegrino. He prayed; the gallery responded.

A videotape, of priests taking the shroud casket from the shroud altar and then lifting the shroud from the casket, was shown, as well as a reconstruction of the probable 2,000-year history of the shroud itself. Pope Paul VI, who rarely allows himself to appear on television, spoke for eight minutes by videotape. And that was that.

Austria, Belgium, Portugal, and Spain, by way of their national television systems, brought the program to their populations. As a consequence, perhaps as many as 200 million viewers saw the show, the largest audience ever assembled for a shroud exposition. They had sat through thirty-five minutes of pious devotion to what must have seemed to many of them, who had never heard of the shroud, to have been nothing more than a religious cloth with a strange painting on it.

Clearly, to the sindonologists who had come to Turin for the exposition, it was a disappointment. True, they had gotten to see the relic firsthand and true, more people than ever before had gotten to see the shroud; but the scientific aspects of the shroud were never mentioned. The Turin authorities later admitted that they had deliberately omitted them because they didn't want controversy to mar the religiousness of the event. Even the positive-negative aspect of the images on the cloth—the one thing that set the shroud apart from all other ancient artifacts and relics—was glossed over.

"The distinct impression left was more reverential than enlightening," said Father Rinaldi immediately after the presentation was over.

No sindonologist he'd talked to since the telecast, said Dr. Judica-Cordiglia a day later, was satisfied with what had gone on the air. Judica-Cordiglia apparently was a member of the secret 1969 commission, and he was disappointed that he hadn't been consulted about the format of the program.

Paul VI was not the first pope to praise the shroud. Between 1472 and 1480 Sixtus IV issued four bulls indicating that he believed the shroud to be worthy of the highest veneration. In 1506, Julius II proclaimed the "feast of the Holy Shroud," with its own mass and office, for the town of Chambery, France, where the shroud was located at the time. In 1582, after the shroud had gone to Turin, Gregory XIII extended the feast to the entire realm of the House of Savoy. Since Savoia extended at that time into France and the diocese of Troyes, mass was being celebrated in the very diocese where, two hundred years before, the shroud had been denounced as a fake. Between Gregory XIII and Paul VI, nineteen other popes expressed confidence in the authenticity of the shroud.

Most recently, Pius XII, in a message to the First International Shroud Congress held in Rome in 1950, "wished that the participants at the congress contribute ever more zealously to spreading the knowledge and veneration of so great and sacred a relic." John XXIII, on seeing the shroud, was overheard saying, "This can only be the Lord's own doing." And Paul VI, in the course of a homily given during a mass in St. Peter's Basilica, June 1967, said, "Perhaps only the image from the holy shroud reveals to us something of the human and divine personality of Christ." ∎

The 1973 exposition on Eurovision

Top   **The shroud in the Hall of the Swiss** (RKW)
Bottom   **The cardinal's face superimposed on an orphan present in the Hall of the Swiss** (RKW)

Top   **Pope Paul reading his address** (RKW)
Bottom   **The face of the man in the shroud as it appeared on the television screen.** (RKW)

En route to Paris

The day after the exposition I left Turin. I was disappointed, but not discouraged. I had gotten what I came for—and indeed a good deal more. I'd had a firsthand look at the Turin authorities in whose inept, if well-meaning, hands the shroud rests. I saw the shroud itself, an experience worth far more than contemplating the photographs. And I bought a set of the color photographs of the shroud, taken in 1969 by Giovanni Battista Judica-Cordiglia.

Paris was the first stop on my itinerary. There I hoped to find some new information on the fabric of the shroud.

After studying blowups of the 1931 Enrie photographs, textile experts were able to say that the shroud was made of linen woven from flax, a wiry long-stemmed plant that grows best and most abundantly in sandy, temperate zones like Palestine. The flaxen threads, which appear coarse and were probably handspun, correspond to the No. 50 and No. 70 threads of the present-day English flax count. The pattern of the weave was an overall herringbone twill, broken at intervals by a forty-thread stripe.

Linens woven in 4000 B.C. can be seen in Egyptian museums; twill weaves existed long before the birth of Christ. But why wasn't there an example of herringbone twill dating back just 2,000 years? A relatively sophisticated loom would have been needed to do the job, some experts believed, and such a loom could easily have been invented by the time of Christ. Egyptian murals showing looms almost as advanced as required date back 4,000 years, other experts countered, and 2,000 years was more than enough time for loom technology in Palestine to develop a sophisticated herringbone twill. ■

Paris

MY FIRST STOP in Paris was the Musée Guimet, a medium-sized building housing a special collection of Oriental artifacts. According to a plaque inside the front door, the museum was founded in 1879 and became part of the Louvre complex in 1945.

At the front desk I asked to see the Gayet collection. Yes, a curator said, there had been an archeologist named Gayet; yes, he had directed excavations in Egypt near Antinoe around the turn of the century; yes, the excavations had been financed by Emile Guimet. . . .

"Is there any chance of my seeing the collection today?" I interrupted.

"No," he said. "At least not here at the Musée Guimet. The Gayet collection has been transferred to the main Louvre building."

"How far away is that?" I asked.

"About a mile."

I headed for the door.

"Try the Coptic section of the Egyptian collection," he called after me.

Msgr. Pietro Savio, the aged Vatican archivist and an apparently indefatigable sindonologist, mentioned the Gayet collection in a pamphlet on the textile aspects of the shroud.

What was especially impressive to Savio was the variety of sophisticated weaving patterns, the herringbone among them, dating back to approximately A.D. 130.

"The weaving industry was large-scale and fundamental to the economic and social life of Egypt," wrote Savio. Young people were paid to learn weaving, apprenticeship lasting sometimes as long as five years. The best fiber came from Acaia in the region of Elis. It took, on the average, three men and one woman six days to weave a roll of cloth 98 feet long. The cloth was then boiled—presumably a cleaning process—and then dyed with colors extracted from herbs. Purple apparently was the most fashionable color, with natural "whitened with a kind of soap made from the poppy" as the second favorite. The finished product carried the name of the region in which it was manufactured, the most prized being Pelusium linen, and it was exported to a number of other Mediterranean countries that could afford to pay the price. ■

I had never been to the Louvre before, and so I was unprepared for what I saw looming before me: a U-shaped fortress many football fields long, built on the right bank of the Seine. In 1793, after the French Revolution, it was converted into a museum, which today houses such treasures as the Venus de Milo and the Mona Lisa.

I gave my name and purpose to a guard inside the front door. In a few minutes I was in the department of Egyptian antiquities, which had been started in 1826 to house collections acquired by Napoleon during his Egyptian campaigns. Then I arrived at the office of the Coptic section.

As usual, neither of the two women in the office spoke English. I tried my best to communicate with them in basic English, with gestures, and finally by drawing pictures of corpses with veils over their faces. At last they understood; one of them telephoned her boss and handed the instrument over to me.

It was Pierre Bourguet speaking; he was the curator. Yes, he did speak English. No, he couldn't see me today; it was his day off. After telling him in detail why I had to see him, he said he would make an exception to his usual holiday practice of "no work" and come down. I was to wait in his office.

The reason I was looking for the Gayet collection was that in Turin a British Benedictine had shown me Gayet's *Annals,* a copy of which he happened to have with him, and read me page 134.

"Among these documents," Gayet had written about the shrouds he'd unearthed, "the most important one is a face veil, folded in four, and carrying the impression of the face to which it was applied. These imprints formed something like dark spots where the prominences of the face were, and show up black. According to specialists, they are from the action of the chemicals used in the embalming of the body. This image gives us the face of a dead man."

The passage was accompanied by drawings of two of the bodies that Gayet had dug up. They had been wrapped first in shrouds and then mummy-style, apparently with the face veil having been applied first.

The linen fabric of the shroud woven in a herringbone twill (HSG)

If the reference was correct, then I could locate another shroud with a body imprint and thus dispel the idea that the Turin shroud was unique.

Bourguet arrived an hour and a half later. He was a spry-looking man, bald, smoking a thin brown cigar.

After introductions—I was surprised to learn he was also a Jesuit priest—I asked him if he had ever come across a burial cloth with the impression of a face on it.

"No, never."

"What about the burial cloths in the Gayet collection?"

"I know the Gayet finds, but none of them have the imprint of a face. I'm sure. I would know."

I handed him the page from Gayet's *Annals*.

"It does say that here, doesn't it?" He sounded genuinely surprised. "Apparently there's something to what you say. But I've been through all the Gayet findings, and I've never seen a face veil."

Bourguet read the page from the *Annals* again. He looked at me for a long moment, then said, "It isn't normally done, but in view of the evidence I suppose I should do it."

"Do what?" I asked hopefully.

"If you'll come back tomorrow, I'll take you back into the storage room where they keep the reserves. You and I will go through all of Gayet's things, and that way we'll know for sure."

Of course I agreed to come back, and I thanked him for his courtesy.

Back at the hotel, I decided to brush up on the French sindonologists of the last eighty years, the most famous of whom was surely Paul Vignon.

As a young man in the 1880s Vignon liked to caper about the ridges and ravines of the French Alps; but this was not without its psychological as well as physical risks; he had a nervous breakdown. In the year of recovery that followed he took up painting, which turned out to be not only excellent therapy but which also revealed a hidden talent. On release from the hospital, he decided to turn toward his second love, biology, and in 1897 joined the staff of the magazine *Biology Year*.

When Secondo Pia's photographs of the shroud appeared in French newspapers and magazines the following year, Vignon felt the fascination of both artist and scientist. He wondered how such images had been transferred to the linen of the shroud, and during the course of the next several decades he developed his theories.

At first, he thought the images might have been painted on the shroud. The artist would have had to know how to paint in reverse shading—that is, to paint the opposite of what is seen in normal light. Vignon concluded that any attempt at such a feat centuries before the concept of positive and negative images had been developed was just about inconceivable.

Even if an artist had the genius and the know-how, how could he have checked his work? And how could anyone else have been able to appreciate it? In both cases, the artist would have needed the positive and negative images photography produced. Why would he go to all the trouble to produce an image that would not be intelligible to those who saw it? And what could possibly motivate him to do a painting like this?

Perhaps there was another possibility. Perhaps the negative images on the shroud were produced by some natural process. Perhaps wear and tear had caused an inversion in the color of the paints over a period of time; perhaps heat had done the trick over a short period of time.

"The flesh tints may have been painted with a mixture of white paint," one critic had written, "which is usually an oxide of lead or of zinc combined with reds (sulphate of mercury), ochers, or naturally tinted earths; the shadows may have been done with black paint mixed with the same ochers and natural burnt earths, or even with bitumen (petroleum). [Then] the Holy Shroud passed through critical periods, such as the fire in 1532, when the constitution of its colors must have been considerably modified . . . the [light] bitumen burnt . . . [and] turned dark because of contamination of the atmosphere."

Origin of image:
The painting theory

Shortly after the 1898 exposition, two Italian artists, Carlo Cussetti and Enrico Reffo, were commissioned to re-create with paint on canvas the images and marks they saw on the shroud; when finished, the two replicas were photographed. The film negatives on the opposite page—Cussetti's on the top, Reffo's on the bottom—have a totally different quality from the film negative of Secondo Pia's facial image (below).

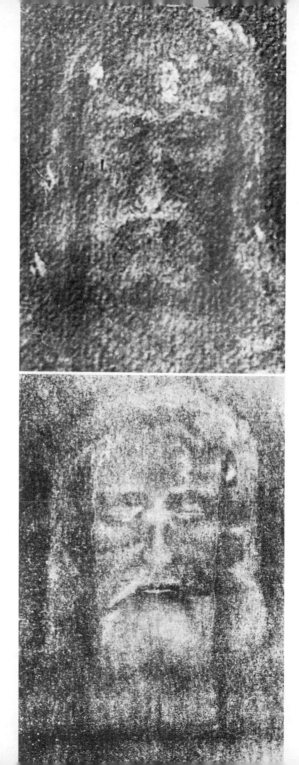

All such theories, however, depended on one essential fact: the presence of paint on the cloth. On examining the photographs with a magnifying glass, Vignon couldn't find a trace of paint. Moreover, when he himself painted a portrait on a piece of linen approximating the shroud material and subsequently folded it into a small square, the paint flaked off. If the shroud had been folded and unfolded, rolled and unrolled for at least five centuries, painted-on images just could not have survived.

Dyes were another possibility. If the image had been dyed onto the cloth, it would not have inverted itself into a negative image. And the image appeared to be monochromatic—the color being variously described as brown or rusty red, the light parts being the natural color of the cloth itself. Only in this last instance, which semed most unlikely to Vignon, could the external chemical base of the monochrome have possibly been inverted. ■

Two city blocks, five hundred yards, we walked—Father Bourguet with his secretaries and I with my camera and notebooks—through one hall after another of the Louvre, passing by paintings of crochety men, bosomy women, dreamy cloudscapes, and angry seascapes before we finally arrived in a gigantic room stacked to the ceiling with boxes and trunks. Cold winter air was descending from a hole in the ceiling—the roof was being repaired—and dust rose as Bourguet pulled Gayet's trunks from the wall racks. Dark, moldy, bulky, there were three of them.

We carried the first, coffin-style, to an uncluttered spot under the hole in the ceiling (the light was best there) and opened it. It was full of burial cloths made of heavy, scratchy linen that looked like nightshirts or summer dresses. Actually they were tunics—simple, knee-length garments with sleeves to the elbow, no pleats, a place for the head, and two side seams. Decorations of some sort had been sewn on some of the sleeves and bottom hems.

There were probably seventy-five such tunics in the trunk, together with some modest headdresses and small napkin-sized pieces of cloth. All, according to Gayet, had been used in burying Jesus' followers in Egypt, the Coptic Christians, around the end

This ancient Egyptian burial shroud, dating back to A.D. 130, was photographed in a Louvre Museum warehouse. It clearly shows the stain of decomposition but not the image of the one enshrouded. (RKW)

of the first century. The bodies had been clothed in the tunics, it appeared, wrapped in shrouds like the one in Turin, then wound mummy-style with ribbons of cloth.

Going through the tunics—I was tempted to hold my nose, but after 2,000 years there was no smell—I was immediately struck by the decomposition. Stains, looking like the swirls of what were once oil chemicals, went through the fabric to the other side. I thought I could distinguish bloodstains from decayed-flesh stains, but now I wasn't so sure. The tunics and the napkins had contained bodies all right, but there wasn't one imprint of a body or face. It was as though the bodies had simply melted through the cloth, leaving behind only a hodge-podge of human disintegration.

"You see," said Bourguet as he closed the lid of the first trunk, "nothing."

We moved on to the second trunk and then the third. As he and I paid special attention to the napkins, which were the size of facecloths, the two secretaries ooh-ed and ah-ed over the fabric, commenting excitedly on the weaves and strengths of the ancient linen.

"I didn't think you'd find one," said Bourguet as he closed the lid on the third trunk. "Now at least you know it's not here."

"At least the cloths prove that corpses buried in linen leave behind stains of decomposition," I managed to say.

"Why is that important to know?"

"The shroud of Turin."

"I'm afraid I don't know as much about the shroud as I should."

"Would you mind if I took some photographs of the burial shirts?"

"Of course not. But please hurry before we all freeze to death!"

Vignon's second theory had to do with direct contact of the cloth with the body, and I could not help but think of the theory as I was photographing the undefined whirls and whorls on the Antinoe burial cloths.

Wearing a fake mustache to approximate the face in the shroud, Vignon had lain on a table and had two aides apply

Origin of image:
The contact stain theory

Giuseppe Judica-Cordiglia, professor of forensic medicine at the University of Milan and director of the International Sindonology Center of Turin, obtained these images by smearing the face of a corpse with blood and spices, placing a linen cloth on top, and then photographing the results. The positive is at the top, the negative on the bottom. (HSG)

powdered chalk—red chalk, since that would show up better than white—to his face. The aides then pressed over his face a cloth resembling the shroud in texture, and rubbed. To everyone's surprise, when the cloth was raised, it contained a negative image of Vignon's face; the darks were light and the lights were dark. But the image itself was a disappointment. The eyes, cheeks, and mouth were too low; the nose was flattened. It was at best a caricature, and nothing at all like the precise, well-proportioned face on the linen surface of the shroud.

Twice more the scientists tried the experiment—once using less pressure than the first time; once using more pressure. The results were the same: the chalk contacts were little more than smears.

What had happened, I was to read later, had a logical explanation. "Contact alone could not render on a flat surface a true and undistorted impression of a cylindrical object," wrote John Walsh in his 1963 book on the shroud. "The flat surface would have to be wrapped around the cylinder and on being opened out again would unavoidably enlarge and distort the original object. The disparity would be more apparent where the cylinder's surface was uneven, as in a human face." ■

The body had been in the shroud long enough to form an image on the cloth—no longer than thirty-six hours according to the New Testament—but not long enough for putrefaction to set in.

But how could this be?

As we hurried back to the warmth of Bourguet's office, I could think of only two answers.

Either the body, dead or alive, was taken or stolen from the tomb with the shroud left behind—

Or the body, dead but not having begun to corrupt, became alive again, shed the shroud, and left the tomb.

The one is a logical possibility; the other is a matter of faith.

Vignon's third theory had to do with gases and vapors rising from the body and acting chemically on the shroud in such a way as to produce the body images. He got the idea while reading of the film experiments being conducted by René Colson, a physicist at Paris' *Ecole Polytechnique.* Together they developed a series of hypotheses which they subsequently tested experimentally.

Vignon began with a metal medallion; Colson, with a sculpture of Jesus' head. They dusted the objects with zinc powder and put them in light-tight boxes. Vignon put a film plate under his medallion; Colson put a film plate over his sculpture; the one would check vapors traveling downward; the other, upward. When they developed the plates twenty-four hours later, they saw images—negative images. The medallion was a little out of focus, but the bust in profile was indeed recognizable.

Zinc was obviously not an element in the ointments used in Jewish burials, but perhaps the ointments were not the image-forming agent. Perhaps urea was. Urea is found in the bladder, of course, but it is found also in sweat, morbid sweat. The sweat of a person undergoing a crisis, especially a crisis of pain, would be urea-rich. When it ferments, it would turn into carbonate of ammonia, which in turn would emit ammoniacal vapors.

But how could these vapors make an image on a linen cloth? A paste of myrrh and aloes blended with olive oil—a recipe derived from the Old Testment—they surmised was spread, not directly on Jesus' body, but on the shroud in which the body was wrapped. Aloes consist mainly of two chemical elements: aloin and aloetine, both of which oxidize and darken into a brownish color when they come into contact with alkalies like ammonia.

To test this hypothesis, Vignon and Colson dipped a piece of linen into a mixture of oil and aloes. Then they dipped half of the cloth into ammonia water; this half oxidized, browned, and darkened immediately. When the linen was dried, the oil and aloes on the one half turned to flakes or powder which could easily be brushed off; the stain on the other half was clear and indelible, and the fabric itself had lost none of its suppleness. So far, so good.

The next step was to test the hypothesis with an object. They picked a plaster head-form, saturated it with ammonia water, and covered it with an aloes-impregnated linen cloth. The result was a brown blur on the cloth. Then the two scientists switched to a plaster cast of a hand, onto which they slipped a suede glove larded with the aloes-and-oil mixture. Slowly, carefully, they poured the ammonia water between the cast and the glove. The result on the interior of the glove, when it was slit open, was the image of a hand, not a perfect image, but one to give validity, good enough even today, to the "vapograph theory." ∎

"There's only one more thing you can do," said Bourguet when we arrived back at his office. "Some of the Gayet collection was sent to one of the two museums in Lyons where Monsieur Guimet, the man who financed Gayet, was from. You might go there. I know the curators. I could arrange things for you."

"I might just do that."

"But again, I don't think you'll find this imprinted face veil you're looking for."

"Why not? It, or something quite like it, must have existed in 1902 when Gayet wrote that passage in the *Annals*."

"If it did exist, and because it was such an unusual item, perhaps Guimet gave it away. He was the kind of man who, when somebody appreciated something, would say 'take it.' "

"Perhaps."

"As for Gayet, I know little about him. He may have been perhaps a little misguided, a little anxious, in describing the veil as having the imprint of a face. An archeologist always needs justification for his funding, you know, and maybe Gayet, after a hard day's work, a little wine—"

We both laughed.

"But who am I to speculate on such things," he said with a grin. "If you want to go to Lyons, I'll be glad to make the introductions."

I decided against it.

"I have to be in London tomorrow. Perhaps I'll write to the museums. All I need to know is if they have such a face veil and can they send me a photograph of it."

The decision to write turned out to be a good one. I got letters back from R. de Micheaux, curator of the Musée Historique des Tissues, and Madelaine Rocher-Jauneau, curator of the Musée des Beaux-Arts, saying they were sorry but there were no face veils in their collections of Gayet material. Micheaux went on to say that he would have been surprised if there were, since everything of Egyptian origin "had been sent back to the Louvre." ■

En route from Paris to London

When Kurt Berna, the German sindonologist who blew the secrecy of the 1969 shroud commission, heard that I was researching the shroud with a view to writing a book, he insisted on flying from Stuttgart, Germany, to London, to give me his several theories. On my own flight to London from Paris, I decided to sift through my bag of books and pamphlets to see what I could learn of the man.

First of all, his real name was Hans Naber. For a variety of reasons he occasionally used Kurt Berna and John Reban.

Hans Naber, so far as I could tell, was born a Catholic, but his Catholicism was more a formality than a commitment. In 1936, when he was fifteen, he left school to learn the hotel business from the bottom up. He waited on tables in the restaurants of Europe—he once served Winston Churchill in London—but before he could advance from table waiter to *maître d'hôtel,* Hitler was advancing on Poland.

He was subsequently drafted into the German army, and because he showed a talent for writing, he became reporter-writer for his company, a job which consisted mainly of writing up internal matters for the unit.

Naber was sent to France, and took part in the battles of Normandy. When the German army was thrown into disarray by the advancing Allied armies, he deserted, escaped capture by changing clothes, and made his way back to Stuttgart.

After the surrender, most Germans had to scrounge for the necessities. Naber was no exception; he turned to black marketeering, which made him a modest living until 1947, when Jesus appeared to him in a dream.

Around 4:00 A.M. on February 18, 1947, lying awake in his parents' home, Hans Naber saw on the wall of his bedroom a technicolor "film of the passion." Included in it were scenes of the trial, crucifixion, entombment, resurrection, and ascension. "They were so real," he later told a magazine, "that I was under the impression they were actually happening. It went on for seven days. I couldn't eat or sleep. The only thing I could do was drink water. I couldn't get out of bed."

On the seventh day, with Naber "physically exhausted and on the verge of madness," something even more unusual happened.

"On one wall of my room, at a stroke, a very intense light appeared, and it diffused through the whole room. Within it Jesus appeared. . . . He was tall. . . . He had long hair, a beard, a mustache. . . . It was highly clear light, eerie, but at the same time not blinding, permitting a clear vision of him. He was dressed in a long white tunic, and there were no wounds on his body."

What Jesus said made such an impact on Naber that he picked up a pen and wrote it down as though someone were guiding his hand. In essence the message was as follows:

"I did not die on the cross. . . . The wounds on my hands and feet took away my strength. The pains burned in my body. . . . The beast opened up my side. . . . Its lance was thrust from below into my chest [but] it did not hit my heart. . . . My side bled. . . . My body was lifeless, but not dead. The heart still beat . . . my wounds were anointed with balm . . . Joseph of Arimathea laid me in a grave of rocks . . . my body could rest . . . my heart grew stronger . . . then I rose again."

While Jesus was talking to him as Naber wrote on the paper, Naber could recall each item in vivid close-up, the most vivid of which was Jesus' last words: "I am Jesus whom men crucified. You, Hans, have seen that I did not die on the cross. You must render testimony of this fact." Then Jesus was gone.

Naber slept for three days and, revived from the ordeal, quit the black market and began giving fervent witness to the truth he believed he'd learned. *Neuen Zeitung,* an occupation-army newspaper published by the Americans for German civilians, published an interview with Naber. Most readers didn't take the story seriously; some readers were outraged to think he would challenge the fact that Christ died on the cross.

He needed proof, Naber said, and not long thereafter he heard of the shroud of Turin for the first time. ■

London

WHEN Naber and I met in London the following day, he filled me in on what had happened next. A priest friend gave him a book on the shroud by R. W. Hynek, the Czechoslovakian doctor who had done work on the possible causes of Christ's death. When he came to the chapter stating that all doctors who have studied the shroud photographs at length believe it held a corpse, he stopped.

If the shroud had wrapped a dead man, he realized, then his vision couldn't be true. He would have to admit he'd been imagining things, perhaps even hallucinating. Naber couldn't accept either of these conclusions, so he bought all the books he could find on the shroud, as well as life-size blowups of the 1931 Enrie photographs.

Poring over the apparent bloodstains on the shroud, he told me, he suddenly recalled an incident in the war. "It was in 1942. On the home front. There'd been an automobile accident in which a man in our company had been killed. As the company writer, I was to go to the autopsy room and make the report. I was standing there with my sergeant. The doctor made a cut on the man, but no blood came out. I was surprised and asked the sergeant why this was so. He said he didn't know. We asked the doctor, and he said corpses don't bleed. They can bleed a little—a few drops maybe, but not large quantities.

"And so, while I was looking at the shroud pictures and all the blood on the shroud, I remembered what the doctor had said. Corpses don't bleed. And then I realized that there was my proof. The body in the shroud was covered with blood! Yet corpses don't bleed! The body must not have been a corpse. It must still have been alive when put in the shroud. Otherwise, how could the blood have gotten on it? Corpses don't bleed. The heart must still have been pumping when they put Jesus in the shroud!"

Later Naber qualified his statement. Corpses, as the doctor had said, could bleed a little, but not in the amounts shown on the shroud around the scalp and on the hands and arms. Such copious exudations, he said, could only have been pumped out by a living heart.

Still later Naber received confirmation of this theory from another doctor, W. B. Primrose, former senior anesthetist at Glasgow Royal Infirmary. In an article entitled "Jesus's Survival from the Cross," Primrose used, among others, the argument that corpses don't bleed.

> How the blood stained the cloth of the shroud was clearly a mystery. Paul Vignon and Pierre Barbet found, after many attempts, that it was impossible to transfer blood to a linen cloth with anything like the precision shown on the shroud. If the blood were too wet when it came into contact with the cloth, it would spangle or run in all directions along the threads. If it were not wet enough, it would leave only a smudge. The perfect-bordered, picturelike clots on the shroud, it seemed, could not be reproduced by staining. ■

Reflecting on his seven-day vision, Naber made another discovery. He saw the tip of the lance, which had been thrust up into Jesus' side, sticking out of the left pectoral muscle. In other words, according to his vision, the lance tip had not come to rest within the chest cavity as most historical, medical, and theological experts believed; it had emerged several inches above the left nipple. Peering at the pectoral area on his shroud photos, he even thought he could see the tiny wound mark. It was circular and could be differentiated from the marks of the scourging, which were straight and smaller.

By drawing a straight line from the point of entry on the right side between the fifth and sixth ribs (which was Barbet's hypothesis and which was quoted by Hynek) through the lungs to the exit wound at the left pectoral muscle, Naber had what appeared to be a lance-path that missed the heart. He promptly went to a hospital where he had an X-ray taken with a simulated lance laid across the course he'd plotted. The result was a negative of his chest cavity with a lance-path that missed the top of his heart by approximately three inches.

Now there was no question in his mind that his vision had been correct in all of its details. He began to search for other supporting evidence, especially in the Scriptures. "Nowhere in the Old Testament does it say that the Messiah had to die, or would die, on the cross," he said, and in support of this he cited verses from the fifty-third chapter of Isaiah. Nor did the New Testament indicate that Jesus wanted to die; and he cited the thirty-ninth verse, the twenty-sixth chapter, of Matthew.

Salvation came at the ascension, theologized Naber. The resurrection was really just a resuscitation. Christ may have appeared dead when he was taken from the cross, but in reality he was still alive. His breathing and other life signs may have stopped, but enough oxygen was still circulating in his blood to keep vital centers, such as the brain, alive. Once in the tomb, the calm allowed him to revive.

By the mid 1950s Hans Naber ran into stiff opposition in trying to get his theories accepted in Germany. "Purest fantasy" is what Werner Bulst called them; he was a Jesuit priest and professor of fundamental theology at a Catholic college in Frankfurt, and one of the few scholars in Germany at the time writing in support of the shroud's authenticity. ■

In 1954, Naber told me, he put his theories into book form, calling it *The Fifth Gospel*. He managed to borrow money to get it printed, and sent copies to the Vatican. The average German reader, however, refused to buy the book; it was a flop.

Around 1955, Naber met a seventy-five-year-old pathologist from Cologne who agreed with his theories. Hirt was the profes-

Cause of death theories

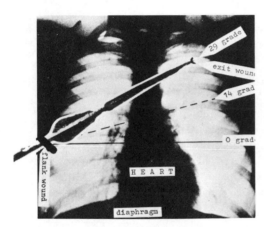

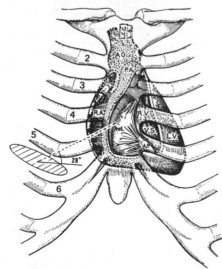

Left **Hans Naber's self-controlled chest X-ray illustrating that the lance would have missed the heart** (HN)
Below **Dr. David Willis' diagram showing that the lance would have hit the heart** (DW)
Opposite, top **Barbet's death theory** (DW)
Opposite, center **Moedder's death theory** (DW)
Opposite, bottom **Sava's death theory** (DW)

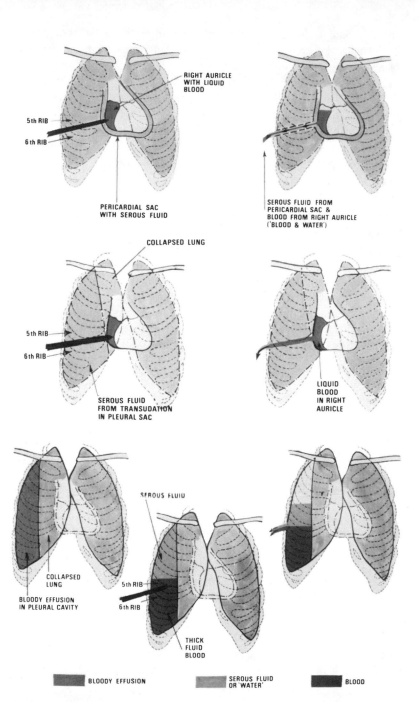

RIGHT AURICLE WITH LIQUID BLOOD

5th RIB

6th RIB

PERICARDIAL SAC WITH SEROUS FLUID

SEROUS FLUID FROM PERICARDIAL SAC & BLOOD FROM RIGHT AURICLE ('BLOOD & WATER')

COLLAPSED LUNG

5th RIB

6th RIB

SEROUS FLUID FROM TRANSUDATION IN PLEURAL SAC

LIQUID BLOOD IN RIGHT AURICLE

SEROUS FLUID

COLLAPSED LUNG

BLOODY EFFUSION IN PLEURAL CAVITY

5th RIB

6th RIB

THICK FLUID BLOOD

BLOODY EFFUSION   SEROUS FLUID OR 'WATER'   BLOOD

sor doctor's name; Naber couldn't remember his Christian name. Together they created "The German Convention for the Shroud of Jesus" in 1956 and from that time on Naber would refer to this "convention" as a body of scientists who agreed with his findings.

By 1960 Naber had written a second book and published three profusely illustrated magazines. At first glance these magazines could easily have been mistaken for European editions of well-known mass-market periodicals, so professionally and glossily had they been put together. A glance at the mastheads inside, however, identified him as editor-publisher.

Waging a campaign against what he considered falsehood in Naber's writings, Werner Bulst wrote in 1960: "An uninformed reader might perhaps treat as important the fact that in his reports [Naber] frequently refers to well-known authorities such as Prof. Dr. Von Campenhausen [Professor of Protestant theology at Heidelberg], Prof. Dr. Siegmund [Catholic theologian of Fulda], and Prof. Dr. Reisner [a physician from Stuttgart]. Personally questioned [however], all declared that they had no connection with Berna or his ideas." ■

Around 1960, Naber told me, he met a rich banker. He wouldn't identify the man other than to say he was a jeweler from Switzerland who believed that Naber's theories were a possible bridge between Jews and Christians. If Jesus hadn't died on the cross, so this man's thinking went, then the Jews couldn't be blamed for his death. This immediately became a recurrent theme in Naber's writing.

Another person who believes that the shroud will unite the world's religions is the famous psychic forecaster Jeane Dixon.

"The evidence of the shroud is so extraordinary—and scholars have shown already that it is neither a hoax nor a painting—that I feel it will have an impact on religious life like the Dead Sea scrolls or the finding of the true cross.

74

"I believe the shroud is destined to become a rallying point for all religions," she was quoted as saying in the June 30, 1974 issue of *The National Enquirer.*

"I see it bringing people of all faiths and creeds into a deeper faith. It will heal all our souls—and will be the biggest thing in religion since the Crusades. ■

In 1964 Naber founded "The International Foundation for the Holy Shroud." He refused to reveal the foundation's membership, he said, because they would be subject to unfair attacks from powerful Catholic sources; but he did use the foundation to raise money for his work.

The next year, under the name of Kurt Berna, he published a book entitled *Inquest on Jesus Christ;* it was subsequently translated into English and published in London. The success and notoriety for which he had been working eighteen years came suddenly. A UPI wire story, dated November 22, 1967, flashed his story around the world. Soon, in addition to the one in Stuttgart, he opened offices in London and Zurich.

In "Did He Die on the Cross?" an essay in a 1967 issue of the *Ampleforth Journal,* a British Benedictine publication, Dr. David Willis took vehement issue with several of Naber's theories. Willis was a doctor himself, latest in a long line of distinguished British physicians. In the seventeenth century one of his great grandfathers, Thomas Willis, was credited with having discovered diabetes and having given his name to that arterial network at the base of the brain now known as the circle of Willis.

With regard to corpses bleeding after death, Willis quoted in the course of his essay Dr. Derek Barrowcliff, British Home Office pathologist: "It can be demonstrated in the mortuary that a short stab wound or cut on the back of the scalp comparable with the wounds made by the crown of thorns . . . or indeed a cut into any dependant part, will bleed freely, continuously, unimpeded by any of the natural mechanisms such as spasm of blood vessel or clotting of the blood which in the living would tend to arrest bleeding. Blood will flow from an open vein as long as the normal laws of gravity operate upon the hydrostatic pressure."

As for the lance missing the heart, Willis said that Naber had calculated incorrectly the exact location of the entrance wound. "It is meaningless to say a wound is in the space between the fifth and sixth ribs without qualification because there can be a difference of 6–7 inches in height between the front and back of the space due to the downward slope of the ribs. The entrance wound as it appears on the shroud is clearly at the front of the rib slope," asserted Willis, "and if Naber had only realized that, his simulated spear thrust would definitely have hit the heart."

With regard to a photograph used in Naber's *Inquest on Jesus Christ,* Willis charged forgery. The anatomical diagram of an adult human heart which Naber had used was in reality the diagram of a young child's chest cavity. The reason why the Naberian spear would have missed such a heart is that the organs were not fully grown.

"The piercing of the heart," Willis went on to say, "is irrelevant because the executioners—Roman soldiers trained in the art of using their weapons and well qualified to know when death had ensued—were convinced that their work was complete in the case of his companions; otherwise they would have broken Christ's legs as they did in the case of the two robbers. The piercing of Christ's side, then, was in the nature of a *coup de grâce,* not the finishing off of someone half dead."

Following the appearance of the Willis essay, Naber admitted in interviews that several of the photographs in *Inquest on Jesus Christ* had been retouched. On photographs of the blood he had darkened the stain considerably, thus adding to the credibility of his theories. He hadn't done it to deceive anybody, he said; the original blood on the body, and indeed on the shroud, must have been much darker, and he wanted the photographs in *Inquest* to conform to what actually had once been the case.

Also in 1967 his foundation came under attack by the United States for mailing a brochure with an appeal for money to a women's organization in Trenton; the women turned it over to the Better Business Bureau of Central New Jersey, who, with the aid of the chancery office of the diocese of Trenton, queried Swiss church officials. The reply from Zurich was anything but flattering; it called the International Foundation for the Holy Shroud "a hoax." ■

I have already explained what Naber did in 1969 to uncover the secrecy of the 1969 shroud commission. When I asked him who his unnamed source was at the time, he said he couldn't reveal it.

If 1969 was the zenith of Naber's credibility, then 1971 was the nadir. He was charged with defrauding creditors of $75,000. "You must make a difference between the foundation and this charge. In the early 1960s I wanted to publish another book. But because no one would publish it because it was against the Church, I had to publish it myself. I had to raise the money. There were about twenty investors. I told them the book was going to be a big seller. But it didn't sell so good and the publishing house I set up—it was a little publishing house—it went broke. Afterward, the investors said I was not talking correctly with them. Maybe I did not say the risk, but how could I know the press wouldn't review my book. It was big stuff, but they wouldn't print anything about it."

He said he had tried to pay the money back, but one of the investors had him arrested. In 1972 he was found guilty of the charges of fraud and was sentenced to two years in prison; he appealed the decision.

The 1972 Summer Olympics, held at Munich between August 26 and September 11, gave Naber an unhoped-for chance to air his views to the world. "Dear Sirs at the foreign press: attention! Germany has secret press censorship!" These were the first words of numerous packets he sent to the Olympiad Press Center. "You are now in a perfectly organized country ... so perfectly organized that discoveries of world significance, which were made in Germany, have now been censored in the German press for over 16 years and therefore not printed! Tell your country not only about the sport but also about the country and people you encounter here. Here are the facts."

No stories about him and/or the shroud seem to have emanated from Munich during the games. Even if the packets had elicited the attention of some of the journalists, the events of September 5 would have overshadowed them: eleven members of the Israeli team were killed by "Black September" terrorists, and news of the tragedy and its aftermath were headlines for days after.

Like Bulst in the 1960s, I had trouble confirming Naber's arguments from medical and biblical authority. Naber was most reluctant to give me names and addresses, and when he did relent, I had little luck. Letters to the radiologist in Stuttgart who backed his claim that the spear would not have entered the heart, to the professor at the University of Tubingen who said that corpses don't bleed, and to the British publisher of *Inquest on Jesus Christ* were either returned, "addressee unknown," or went unanswered. The only one who replied was W. B. Primrose, the anesthesiologist from Glasgow; he still felt corpses don't bleed.

Naber is not the only one who believes that the Gospel account of Jesus' death and burial did not tell all, but that the shroud itself is an authentic relic from the tomb. In *The Passover Plot,* which became an international bestseller, biblical scholar Hugh Schonfield maintained that Jesus did indeed die on the cross but that his body was snatched from the tomb rather than resurrected. That was in 1965. But in 1931, in a foreword to an obscure book written after the exposition that year, Schonfield had this to say about the shroud. "To show that the records are not wholly silent on its earlier wanderings, and that if historical confirmation of its authenticity is needed, the shroud of Turin has one of the best claims of consideration that could be demanded of such a venerable relic." ■

Hans Naber in the Shroud Chapel, St. John's Cathedral, Turin (HN)

What is one to think of Hans Naber? The road he chose to take from 1947 to the present appears to have been one, not so much of deceit, as of a fierce belief that what he had seen in his vision was right and of his overzealousness in trying to make others realize it. The obsession eventually stripped him of family and friends, threw him into collaboration with mysterious figures, and in the end turned him into a three-hundred-pound fat man facing bankruptcy and jail.

I next wanted to meet Leonard Cheshire, the man who had brought Josie Wollam to Turin in 1955 in search of a miracle. An appointment had been arranged, but when I called to confirm it, I learned that he was out of town. An aide of his said that Cheshire had written to cancel the appointment, but unfortunately the letter had never caught up with me.

It was a clear morning over Nagasaki, Japan, on August 9, 1945. Clear, that is, until the bomb exploded. A blinding white flash. An eerie purple glow. A mushrooming fire-cloud. A B-29 banking sharply and heading home. In that plane was Leonard Cheshire, Churchill's personal representative at the dawn of atomic warfare. He would return to England to tell about the bomb that killed eighty thousand people so that hundreds of thousands might live.

As a bombing expert and crack pilot, Cheshire was one of the RAF's "dambusters," pilots who volunteered to fly at low levels through almost impenetrable flak to drop 12,000- to 15,000-pound bombs on pinpoint targets like the submarine pens at Le Havre and Boulogne. For these and other deeds of courage and leadership, he was eventually awarded the Victoria Cross, the Distinguished Service Order, and the Distinguished Flying Cross.

After the war, he decided to steer his life into what he felt was a more meaningful course. With a group of ex-servicemen he organized a self-sustaining community. With nothing but brotherhood as its bond, and with little agreement as to their general focus, the community soon went broke; its members departed, and Cheshire himself fell ill.

Leonard Cheshire with Josephine Wollam in 1955 (LC)

To recuperate he went to the Canadian Rockies, and some time during his convalescence he underwent a religious experience, which he is said to have described as awe at the wonderfulness of creation.

Returning to England, he decided to open a home for the terminally ill. His first patient was Arthur Dykes, who was dying of cancer. They became good friends, talked religion incessantly, and when Dykes finally died, Cheshire, arguing from the laws of aerodynamics to the doctrines of theology, decided to become a Catholic.

That was 1948. By the mid-1950s, encouraged by support from the press and donations from the people, he incorporated as "Mission for the Relief of Suffering" and opened two more homes. Once again he overworked and fell ill, this time with tuberculosis. He was confined to a sanatorium for eighteen months, where he saw, affixed to the wall of his room, the man in the shroud. ■

In Cheshire's absence, John Messent offered to meet with me. He was a good friend of Cheshire's and said he could fill me in on the details of Cheshire's life. Messent joined me late one afternoon after coming from his job as deputy clerk of London's Metropolitan Water Board.

Recuperating at the sanatorium, Cheshire contemplated the man in the shroud. He had read a pamphlet on the shroud written by an American and had found the scientific facts intriguing. He grew to feel that his new-found ministry and the shroud had something in common; both dealt with suffering —the one to relieve it, the other to make its significance understood. He decided to write a pamphlet himself, one aimed specifically at the English reader.

He decided also, on his discharge from the hospital, to buy a bus and convert it into a mobile shroud museum. From G. Enrie he ordered an enlargement of the positive of the frontal view of the body; when it arrived from Turin, he had it enlarged to life-size and installed it over a light panel on the floor of the bus. He then wired an amplifier that would play

Gregorian chant and hung cages for doves that could be released at appropriately pious moments. With these and other sindonological paraphernalia he embarked on a tour of England, lecturing on the relic and giving away copies of his pamphlet.

Churchmen may have winced at Cheshire's tactics, but newspapermen rejoiced at the war hero who had been charmed by a religious relic. HOLY SHROUD GIVES SILENT WITNESS IN LONDON ran one headline. V.C. TELLS THE STORY OF THE SHROUD read another. During the week before Easter 1954, two thousand Londoners passed through the bus, and ten thousand copies of the free pamphlet had been scooped up.

Cheshire himself wrote a story for *The Daily Sketch;* "I Saw the Face of Christ" was bannered across two pages. In addition to recounting the pertinent facts, he wrote that he was more impressed with the shroud than with the atom bomb. The shroud may look like just another portrait, and the bomb appeared destined to change the course of history; yet the shroud loomed higher on his own horizon because "here at last might lie the secret to world peace." ■

Nottingham

THE NEXT DAY I traveled to Nottingham to visit D. Allen-Griffiths, a seventy-one-year-old secretary of the Holy Shroud Information Center, another of the English groups interested in the shroud. Griffiths had written a book on the shroud, *Whose Image and Likeness?* He was especially helpful in giving me additional details of Cheshire's pilgrimage to Turin with Josie Wollam in 1955.

In reply to my letter asking if he had ever made any inquiries into the shroud's history before the fourteenth century, Cheshire had written the following. "History is unfortunately not my subject, and I have never been quite so interested in this aspect of the shroud; it is the scientific and pictorial evidence that has occupied my attention."

Later I acquired a copy of *The Face of a King,* a pamphlet

about his involvement with the relic written by Vera Barclay; and a copy of his own *Pilgrimage to the Shroud,* which was published in 1956. ■

London

To FIND OUT more about the history of the shroud before the 1350s I planned to call on two people while in London. The first was Fr. Maurus Green; he was the Benedictine who had given me the reference in Gayet's *Annals* in Turin. His father, Charles Green, was a career army officer and amateur sindonologist who had developed the iconography theory already put forth by a Frenchman. According to this theory, the shroud face had been the model for many early Christian icons.

When the elder Green died in 1959, with his manuscript on the subject as yet unpublished, the younger Green, now a parish priest, decided to pick up where his father had left off. In time he came to know as much about the shroud's probable history as any sindonologist alive. And when in 1969 his "Enshrouded in Silence," a lengthy article examining all the evidence contributing to the history of the first millennium of the shroud, was published in *Ampleforth Journal,* he was formally recognized as the foremost expert in this aspect of sindonology.

I called him, and we made an appointment.

As mysterious as the shroud was, the face it displayed was remarkably similar to the traditional Christ-type seen on many ancient icons, the religious paintings of early Eastern Christianity.

The first depictions of Jesus were highly idealized; he was shown as a clean-shaven, innocent youth. Around the sixth century, however, that image changed. He suddenly became a grown man with long hair, beard, and eyes that were abnormally large and ovate. If someone had copied the shroud face, the eyes would have appeared exactly that way.

Art historians don't know exactly why Jesus was depicted in these two contrasting ways. Nowhere in Scripture is there any physical description of Jesus; several apocryphal works do

84

contain some random and contradictory descriptions. Could the shroud, then, have caused the change in the way artists portrayed Jesus? Could it even have been the model upon which the virile icons were based?

It was an intriguing idea, one that was first expounded by Paul Vignon in 1902 and developed by him at book-length in 1939.

Checking the icons in the museums and libraries of Paris, Vignon discovered dramatic evidence that the shroud face and the face on the icons had more than a casual link. Not only did the eyes, nose, and mustache seem the same; but strange marks that were not facial features also appeared on both the shroud and the icons. The most unusual of these is a mark between the eyes, just above the top of the nose. It resembled a **V** with a rectangular box resting on top of it; the box appears to have one of its sides, the side nearest the hairline, missing.

This unusual, nonanatomical mark appeared in several different forms. On the earliest icons, such as the one in the St. Pontianus catacomb in Rome, which dates back to the sixth or seventh century, it appears as the rectangle with one side missing, but it does not have the **V**. On the icons made in the eleventh century, such at the Christ of Daphni in Greece, the mark is more stylized: the rectangular lines have become a teardrop or a pendant.

Of the hundreds of Byzantine icons Vignon examined, 80 percent had the identifying mark between the eyes. Among other points of similarity, Vignon listed the following: no ears; no neck; no shoulders; a "forked" beard; a "truncated" mustache; straight nose; enlarged nostrils; one raised eyebrow; a line across the throat (which is really a wrinkle on the shroud); bruised forehead; abnormally shaded or swollen cheeks. No icon had all these similarities, but all had at least a few.

The earliest icons that Vignon found with shroudlike similarities were copies of the "Image of Edessa," a portrait of Jesus on cloth which was discovered in 544 bricked up in a wall in Edessa, the center of Syrian Christianity. After its discovery, the "true likeness" of Christ, as it came to be known, was the object of great veneration in Byzantium. ■

The iconography theory

From the sixth to the thirteenth centuries, according to Rev. Maurus Green, O.S.B., certain features in the representations of Jesus seem to indicate that the artists drew their inspiration directly or indirectly from the features on the shroud. Green particularly points to (A) the bruise across the forehead; (B) three sides of a square between the eyebrows; (C) V-shape to the bridge of the nose; (D) one raised eyebrow; (E) enlarged nostrils; (F) divided moustache; (G) heavy line under lower lip; (H) gap between this line and the beard; and (I) the line across the throat. Compare these features on the shroud image (opposite) with the corresponding ones on the icons on the following pages.

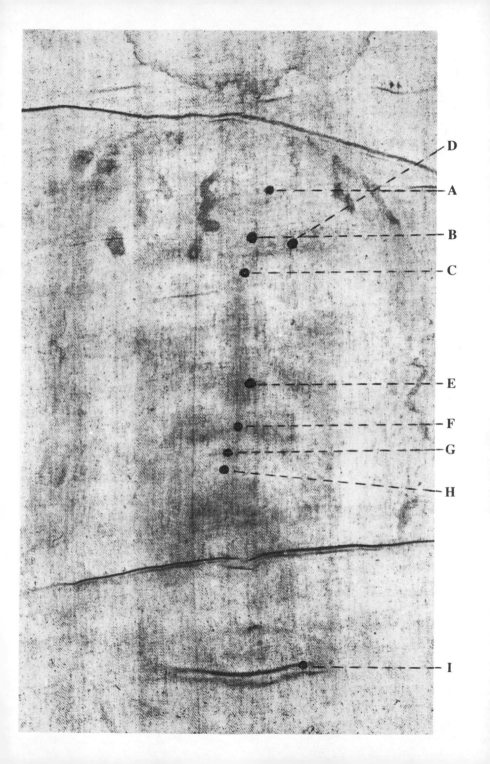

"Edessa must be the key," Fr. Maurus Green said when we met the next day. "If I could search hard enough and a good deal longer, I believe I could come up with more evidence showing that the shroud had been in Edessa. This would give more credence to Vignon's theory, give me something to finish off my father's book, and advance the cause of the shroud in the process.

"There are many representations of Christ, notably the Image of Edessa, which could be derived only from the shroud," Vignon wrote in a 1937 magazine article. "A careful study of these copies, which I recently completed, shows that the . . . face visible on the shroud served as a model for artists as early as the fifth century. The artists did not copy slavishly, but tried to interpret the face, translating the masklike features into a living portrait, which was still a recognizable copy of the original."

In 1938 Vignon published his second book on the shroud. Entitled *The Holy Shroud of Turin Versus Science, Archeology, History, Iconography, and Logic,* it was an updated revision of his 1902 work on the subject. As convincing as the arguments in his book were to many, scoffers at the authenticity of the shroud still pointed to the lack of an unbroken chain of documents attesting to the shroud's existence before 1354. ■

"The more I dug," Father Green went on to say, "the more convinced I became that I would not find any more references to Christ's shroud than had already been uncovered. The documents had been pretty thoroughly sifted. There just didn't seem to be anything substantially new I could find. But the Eastern preoccupation with icons—the preoccupation that caused the exaltation of the Edessan image and gave rise to the subsequent mass of Byzantine Christs—still bothers me. Why had the Eastern Christians been so impressed with images when Christians in the West had been content with relics? It was then that Ian Wilson came along with his intuitive theory: the Edessan image had not been just the first copy of the shroud, as Vignon theorized; it had been the shroud itself!"

Green told me he fought tooth and claw against this theory at

92

first. All scholars know that the Edessan image is only a portrait of Christ; at least that's the way the evidence has always been treated. But then again, he began to realize, it was a cloth and it had been greatly exalted after its discovery. Perhaps the scholars were wrong.

"The more my friend Ian Wilson and I exchanged information on the subject and argued back and forth, the more I realized how this theory might possibly be the missing clue to the puzzle. So many things were pointing to the icon of Edessa. And the more facets I studied, the more probable the theory became."

The theory that the Image of Edessa was the shroud began with legends. In essence, they say that when an early king of Edessa, Abgar V, became mortally ill, he sent for the miracle-worker he had heard about. Jesus did not go to the king himself; instead he pressed a cloth to his face, miraculously leaving his image on it, and sent that back with the king's messenger. The cloth not only healed Abgar; it also converted many of the citizens to Christianity. Shortly thereafter a Roman army invaded the country but the Image of Edessa, as it was now being called, had already mysteriously disappeared.

When the icon was discovered in the wall of the city in 544, it was proclaimed the greatest relic in Christendom. *Acheiropoitos* they called it, a Greek word meaning "not made with hands"; it was also called "The True Likeness of Christ." Placed so as to guard the city, the cloth was said to have miraculous powers in repelling attackers. Eventually it came to be known as the *mandylion,* a Greek word for cloth or veil. Three or four copies of it were made at the end of the sixth century and—after the defeat of iconoclasm, the great movement to destroy images which flourished in Byzantium in the eighth and ninth centuries—the image had spread throughout the empire.

By the tenth century, the image had become so revered that Romanus Lecapenus, emperor of Byzantium, decided he wanted it in the treasure chests of his palace in Constantinople. He sent an army to the gates of Edessa to bargain with the Moslems who were currently occupying the city. The army's

93

instructions were that if they couldn't get the image by bargaining, they were to get it by battle. Outnumbered, the Moslems agreed to relinquish the image in return for two hundred Moslems then being held captive and for twelve hundred silver coins.

The mandylion was brought to Constantinople in 944 amidst great fanfare. Accounts say the cloth was marched triumphantly around the city walls, then taken ceremoniously through the "golden gates" to be lodged permanently in the imperial chapel of Bucoleon. In 1150 the shroud began to be listed among the prizes in the city's treasury; and an anonymous English pilgrim listed the *shroud*—not merely a facial imprint of Christ—as one of the treasures in the emperor's chapel. There are also two recorded references— one made in 1171 and the other in 1201—to the *shroud* in the Bucoleon Chapel. In 1204 the Fourth Crusade sacked Constantinople, and the Image of Edessa disappeared again. ■

Green said that he happened upon three pieces of documentary evidence indicating that the Image of Edessa also had a body imprint on it.

"That changed the situation considerably," he said.

"The first document is a reference from a sermon about the Edessan Image believed to have been given by Pope Stephen III, who was elected to the papacy in 769." The text of the sermon, by the way, appears in a copy made sometime between the ninth and the twelfth century.

The sermon first says, in a passage that may have been added long after the pope's death, that the image impressed on the cloth is Jesus' body. "For the same mediator between God and men . . . stretched his whole body on a cloth, white as snow, on which the glorious image of the Lord's face and the length of his whole body was so divinely transformed that it was sufficient for those who could not see the Lord bodily in the flesh to see the transfiguration made on the cloth."

Then the sermon identifies the body imprints on it as the Image of Edessa. "This cloth, despite the passage of time, remains incorrupt in Mesopotamia Syria in the city of Edessa in the house of the great church."

Green said the second and third documents are references from twelfth-century authors. In 1142 Ordericus Vitalis, discussing the origin of the icon of Edessa, wrote the following: "Abgar reigned as Toparch of Edessa; to him the Lord Jesus sent . . . a most precious cloth, with which he wiped the sweat of his face and in which shone the image of the same savior marvellously depicted; which exhibited to the onlookers the likeness and extent of the body of the Lord."

A short time later Gervase of Tilbury, in discussing a letter Jesus is alleged to have sent Abgar, quoted Jesus as saying: "I send you a cloth in which the figure of my face and my whole body are contained."

"These are just fragmentary references, of course," said Green, "and not very impressive by themselves. Vitalis and Gervase are generally considered by most medieval historians to be gossipers. But then Ian Wilson found the only official history of the Edessan Image ever commissioned, had it translated into English, which had never been done before, and again, the results were supportive of the theory that the image and the shroud are one and the same."

De Imagine Edessena, as the history was entitled, was written by a member of the court of the tenth-century emperor, Constantine Porphyrogenitus, shortly after the image arrived in Constantinople. Its pertinence to the shroud comes in a short description of how the image on its surface appeared to be composed: ". . . a moist secretion without any coloring or artificial aid."

"Clearly," said Green, "this brings us very close to the same apparent characteristic of the Turin shroud.

"Ian has also highlighted the importance of an incident recorded in 944," continued Green, "when the emperor's sons had a special viewing of the image. To the sons it seemed blurred, but Porphyrogenitus was an artist; he was able to make out the portrait clearly. Something of the subtlety of the Turin shroud's stain image is again suggested here."

"But if this were all so," I asked, "why had all the references to the Edessan Image almost overwhelmingly indicated that it had nothing more than a facial image on it? And why had so many copies of it shown nothing more than a facial image on it?"

"Good questions," said Green.

In researching and attempting to advance Vignon's iconography theory in the mid-1950s, Green's father, Col. Charles Green, was thrown out almost bodily from a London museum when he mentioned the shroud.

"Having discovered the Byzantine expert [in the museum]," his father wrote in a letter, "I secured an interview. . . . An incredibly learned young man . . . gave me a list of books [with which to acquaint myself with the field]. . . . When I told him [that I was after a possible link with the shroud] he assured me I would get nowhere. 'Nothing is known of the shroud before the fourteenth century' [he said]. When I told him enough to show him [he was wrong], the change in him was remarkable. From friendliness to contempt. . . . He refused to shake hands with me and ushered me out. I am quite certain he was a bitter anti-Christian and realized that here was something which might revive the old superstition." ■

"Did the Image of Edessa have body imprints on it?" was the question I had asked Ian Wilson when I first met him in Turin. He was an Oxford history graduate and an enthusiastic sindonologist.

Wilson replied to the effect that a Greek liturgical text of the tenth century told how the cloth was so highly venerated and so closely guarded that few were ever allowed to view it directly. The cloth was kept in a casket—a very similar sort of thing that the shroud is kept in now—and people were allowed to see this casket only through a grille—again, very similar to the situation of the shroud today. Only on very solemn feast days was the archbishop allowed to open the casket and see the image for himself. Nobody else was allowed to open it. It was never there for just anybody to see, as it were. And these would have been just the circumstances for the full-length figure to remain secret.

Further, Wilson went on to say, another text refers to the mandylion as having been "doubled in four." He said he took a full-length photograph of the shroud, doubled it in four, and the result was that only the head showed. "If that's how the image was folded," he said, "then even if the entire casket were opened, no one could have seen the body image."

"There's another piece of evidence," Green told me in Turin. "The Byzantine liturgical cloths called *epitaphioi*. The still-surviving epitaphioi are liturgical aids dating from the thirteenth century that have the dead and reclining Christ embroidered on their surfaces. Many of them have the figure in the exact same position as the one on the shroud. Jacques Grimaldi, writing in Latin in 1618, suggests that the earliest epitaphioi were known as far back as the eighth century."

"Once the Edessan Image reached Constantinople in 944," said Wilson, "the evidence that it and the shroud are the same increases. Both Christ's burial garments and the Edessan Image are said to have been kept in the Bucoleon Chapel. In 1201 a palace priest, Nicholas Mesarites, indicated that one of the relics kept in the Bucoleon shows the naked body of Christ. And then in 1204, Robert de Clari, the chronicler of the Fourth Crusade, the one that leveled Constantinople, wrote that he had seen the shroud of Christ in the city and that it had the imprints of his entire body on it."

And then there are the Vitalis and Tilbury references, I thought.

Were the Image of Edessa and the shroud of Constantinople the same? And were they both the same as the shroud of Turin?

No one can be sure, it seems.

What finally clinched things for Green was a comparison of the shroud of Turin with the 'Holy Face of Laon,' a mandylion painted around 1200, perhaps directly from the Image of Edessa. (See photograph on page 91.) The Holy Face of Laon seems to prove to Green that it was inspired by the shroud face and therefore that the artist knew the shroud face well, whenever he saw it.

The chief difficulty with this theory, everyone admitted, is that both the Edessan Image and the burial cloth of Christ are sometimes mentioned as separate and distinct entities on the same lists of relics in twelfth- and thirteenth-century Constantinople. The difficulty can be explained away, said Wilson, by suggesting that the Edessan Images mentioned in the lists are just copies of the original and that therefore the original, which would have the body imprints on it, could have been what the lists referred to as the shroud.

"If Wilson is right," Green would say to me, "we will not only have solved the mystery of the Turin shroud's whereabouts during the first millennium, we will also have a most remarkable account of its by-no-means-inconsiderable place in Byzantine history."

"If you both are right," I said, "then only one historical mystery remains. What happened to the shroud between the time it disappeared in Constantinople in 1204 and reappeared in Lirey, France, around 1356?"

The answer, it seems, has to do with the Knights Templar.

The Knights Templar, as I later learned, were a religious and military order that had been started by a small group of Crusaders in Jerusalem around 1119. Eight or nine of the knights who had been fighting in the Holy Land decided to drop out of their individual armies and form a religious order. Tired of the secular lives they had been leading, they took, in addition to a vow to protect pilgrims from attacks by marauding Moslems, vows of poverty, chastity, and obedience, and adopted as their dress the white surcoat with the red cross in the middle. They pooled all their possessions, and gave a tenth of everything they acquired to the poor. They swore to take on no fewer than three foes apiece in any one battle.

Apparently, other knights and mercenaries in increasing numbers felt the same way as the original founding group had, because within fifty years the order had become a large and powerful army. Money poured in through both dowries of new members and fees for their martial services; little money trickled out. No leader of any army dared antagonize them. Within their own fortresses the Templars were practically self-sufficient. In time they became the Western Church's arm in the East, and in 1163 the pope gave them the right to establish their own clergy. They became like a nation unto themselves.

Toward the end of the twelfth century, however, things

changed. The founding knights had all died. The vows of war and chastity were still sworn to, but the order's wealth was being invested in real estate all around the Mediterranean world: in Jerusalem, Tripoli, Antioch, and Cypress in the East; in Spain, France, Portugal, and England in the West. "At their peak," wrote one historian, "the Templars owned and administered seven thousand manors and estates in Europe."

By 1200 the Templars were the dominant power in the Middle East. Their strongholds along the African coast and on up through the underbelly of Europe were said to be impenetrable. They established friendly ties with some of the Arab armies. Some Moslems even trusted the Templars enough to bank their valuables in the Templar strongholds. And in 1204 the armies of the Fourth Crusade sacked Constantinople.

The question is, Was the Image of Edessa, the shroud of Constantinople, the shroud of Turin, one of the spoils of war? ∎

"I've found no direct evidence linking the Templars to the shroud," Ian Wilson told me in Turin, "but I do have three pieces of circumstantial evidence."

First, in 1307, the Templars, too strong and independent for the European monarchs' taste, were brought to their knees. The king of France had all the Templar leaders in his realm arrested on the charge that they secretly worshipped a mysterious idol "in the form of the head of a man with a long, reddish beard." The idol was never found, but Wilson said he couldn't help but see a resemblance in that description to the face on the Turin shroud.

Second, a painted head, believed to have been a replica of the idol the Templars might have worshipped, was found on the site of an old Templar monastery in England. "It's resemblance to the shroud face is unmistakable!"

Third, as a result of the purges in Europe, three Templar leaders were burned at the stake. Among the last two to be incinerated was a French Templar named Geoffrey deCharnay. It was in another Geoffrey de Charny's church in Lirey that the shroud had come to light fifty years later in 1354. Although the last names of the two Geoffreys were sometimes spelled differently, Wilson said he believed they were related.

"What about the d'Arcis memorandum?" I asked Wilson. "What explanation do you have for that?" The memorandum I was referring to was written in 1389 by Bishop Pierre d'Arcis; in it he said that the shroud exhibited at Lirey around 1356 was a painted fake.

"The whole d'Arcis affair was just a big mistake. The bishop was a sincere man, but he misinterpreted the facts."

When deCharnay was killed at Poitiers, his wife may have put the shroud on exposition with the hope of making a little money. The local clergy probably found it hard to believe that such a tremendous relic could have come into the hands of a modest secular family, and without the Templar around to explain where he got the shroud and exactly what its history was, they branded it a fake.

"I believe that too much effort has been put into discrediting the d'Arcis memorandum," said Wilson. "The truth of the matter is that virtually all his facts were truthful and indeed valuable; it was his interpretation that the shroud was a fake that was misguided."

Beyond that, Wilson wouldn't elaborate. "You'll have to wait for my book to come out," he said.

> The rest of the history of the shroud is a matter of record, and undisputed. The d'Arcis memorandum proved the shroud was still at Lirey in 1389. The imbroglio left the shroud intact, and in 1452 Geoffrey deCharny's granddaughter Margaret sold it to the House of Savoy. ∎

En route from London to New York

So much for the history of the shroud, I thought, as I headed for New York. The textile evidence I had seen so far was convincing. But I was looking forward to talking at some length with the American sindonologists and to doing some investigating on my own on the possible origins of the shroud images.

Esopus

My FIRST STOP in the United States was Mount St. Alphonsus Redemptorist Seminary in Esopus, one hundred miles up the Hudson River from New York City. In a room next to the seminary library is the largest collection of sindonalia in the world outside of Turin. On the walls are life-size (7′ x 4′) photographs of the shroud; on pedestals and tables are pieces of sculpture modeled on the figure in the shroud; and in the bookcases are seven hundred volumes, mostly in French and German, although some sixty are in English. Also in the room are three file cabinets, four drawers apiece, full of uncatalogued notes, articles, manuscripts, and correspondence of the first great American sindonologist, Edward A. Wuenschel.

Wuenschel entered the Redemptorists in 1913, was ordained a priest in 1924, received a doctorate in sacred theology in 1927, and returned to Esopus to teach dogmatic theology shortly thereafter. In the 1930s he was a voluminous writer and much-sought-after lecturer. In 1947 he was appointed rector of the seminary; in 1949 he went to Rome, where he headed the Redemptorist graduate school; in 1960 he became special theological adviser to Francis Cardinal Spellman for the Second Vatican Council, which was to convene in 1962.

When Wuenschel first learned of the shroud in 1934, he was skeptical. After reviewing the evidence, however, he became an ardent supporter of its authenticity. He was the one who, in 1937, arranged for articles to appear in *Scientific American, Reader's Digest,* and *Look.* These presentations of the case for the authenticity of the shroud were not satisfactory in every respect, but they did manage to introduce the shroud to portions of the American public who would not have heard of it otherwise. In the 1940s Wuenschel researched Jewish burial practices and published his results in the *Catholic Biblical Quarterly.* In the 1950s he spent the summers traveling to the European cities important to the history of the shroud and rummaging through bookshops for any and all material concerning it. After his death—he died without ever having seen the shroud—his notes and acquisitions from this

101

Two American sindonologists:
(left) **Rev. Edward A. Wuenschel, C.Ss.R., and** (above) **Rev. Francis L. Filas. S.J.** (HSG)

time were shipped from Rome to Esopus and form the basis of the Wuenschel Collection at the seminary.

From the files of the Wuenschel Collection, I learned many things, the two most interesting of which were, perhaps, his relationship with an editor at *Scientific American* and his discoveries of what happened to the shroud between 1354 and 1452.

When Wuenschel first wrote to *Scientific American* about the possibility of an article on the shroud and enclosed all the positive scientific evidence in favor of the phenomenon, the letter fell on Albert Ingalls' desk.

Ingalls' special interest was not religion, but the telescope— how to make one, how to grind the lens, how to use it to explore the heavens; by the time of his death in 1958 he had written the article on telescopes for the *Encyclopaedia Britannica,* and a lunar crater had been named in his honor. When he opened Wuenschel's letter, he smiled and rejected it politely with the comment that miraculous intervention of the imprints on the shroud would not be acceptable to his agnosticism, let alone to his magazine.

Undaunted, Wuenschel sent a second letter in which he detailed all the negative arguments against the shroud's authenticity, asked Ingalls to consider them, and expressed confidence that he would find them unconvincing. Wuenschel also promised that the article, if *Scientific American* would publish it, would deal only with natural causes.

Ingalls was impressed enough with Wuenschel's second letter to reread his first. In it he noticed, as if for the first time, the argument from photography which intrigued him as a scientist. He replied to Wuenschel that, although he'd like to commission an article, he couldn't see his way to publishing a piece that would be considered propaganda for the Roman Catholic Church.

Wuenschel wrote back, saying he agreed entirely with the editor's observations. A scientist—Paul Vignon—would write the article, and the verifiable photographs of Giuseppe Enrie would illustrate it. To give Ingalls some idea of the visual

103

impact of the shroud and some hint of his own impartiality, Wuenschel invited him to a lecture featuring the Enrie photographs, which he would soon be giving in the auditorium of St. Vincent's Hospital in Manhattan.

Ingalls accepted, attended, and apparently was impressed enough to read the French original of Paul Vignon's 1902 book on the shroud. On the basis of the photos and the book, he at last badgered his editor in chief into commissioning the shroud article. It would run three pages in the magazine; *Scientific American* would print a disclaimer on the first page of the article; Vignon and Wuenschel would receive a hundred-dollar fee.

When the article finally appeared in the March 1937 issue, it was a great success. The shroud's existence was broadcast to perhaps 100,000 educated American laymen (most of whom were Protestant or agnostic), and Ingalls became an ardent defender of the shroud's authenticity. ■

To get some more information on Albert Ingalls, I telephoned the offices of *Scientific American* and was put through to an editor of the magazine.

"I hope you understand," the editor said, "that *Scientific American* is under new ownership now, and we certainly wouldn't have published that article today. It was nonsense."

"Why?" I couldn't resist asking.

"It's just too much to expect that a piece of cloth supposedly wrapped around a man in the Year One would still be a viable subject today. We have too many ancient cloths from Egypt to know this just couldn't happen."

"Ingalls believed the shroud a viable subject," I countered. "Otherwise, he wouldn't have gone to bat for it as he did."

"I knew Albert Ingalls very well," retorted the editor, "and I don't care what letters you have. I refuse to believe that he would have been responsible for an article like that."

"Have you ever read the article?"

"I read it several times, and I remember reading it as a sixteen-year-old boy and thinking how improbable the whole thing was."

"Have you read anything else on the shroud?"

"I'm familiar with the outlines of the story, and it's not worth exploring further."

Whoever the editor was—I didn't catch his name—he reminded me of the London museum curator encountered by Col. Charles Green.

> Also depicted in Wuenschel's correspondence was the success he'd had in unearthing documentary evidence for the whereabouts of the shroud between 1354 and 1452.
>
> "At Turin there was a woman on the staff who took a ferocious interest in my project and kept on digging up material, the existence of which I did not even suspect.
>
> "It was the same at Chambery. I had a letter of introduction to the Italian consul, who turned out to be the perfect diplomat and got me into the archives with the ease of a Ludwig von Pastor. There I had the whole staff at my command and permission to work in the archives after the closing hour. They also let me take jealously guarded books to my room at the Grand Seminaire.
>
> "At Troyes I struck the best luck of all. I knew the old vicar general. . . . He is one of the leading historians of Champagne . . . as familiar with the local archives . . . as with his breviary, and those are the archives that contain the most important collection of documents on the beginning of the Western career of the shroud—the whole Lirey story and its sequel. . . . What a haul! I was able to do in three or four days what it would have taken months to do in the archives on my own."
>
> What Wuenschel found seemed to validate Ian Wilson's theory of what happened to the shroud from the time it appeared in Lirey in 1354 until it was sold to the house of Savoy in 1452. ■

Brooklyn

WHEN Wuenschel left the United States for Rome in 1949, he left the care of the American shroud movement in the hands of another Redemptorist priest. Adam J. Otterbein, a former student

of his and now a professor of theology at the seminary, was the one who shot the black-and-white photographs at Turin while I was shooting the colored ones. Many was the night the tall, lanky Otterbein had listened to the chain-smoking Wuenschel as he pointed out detail after detail of the fascinating and mysterious relic.

Otterbein took his new assignment seriously, and for the next two years worked hard. On October 6, 1951, Francis Cardinal Spellman, then archbishop of New York, officially decreed the creation of the Holy Shroud Guild at Esopus with Father Otterbein as its director. In December of that year Turin approved the guild as its first North American affiliate of the Cultores Sanctae Sindonis, the parent organization. The guild was now the organization's official representative in the United States, with the responsibility of promoting interest in the relic through the country.

To attract members and inspire donations, the guild published a pamphlet containing all the pertinent facts about the shroud. The pamphlet was a reprint of *The Chalice,* a magazine published by the Confraternity of the Most Precious Blood, an entire issue of which had been devoted to the shroud in 1937. A former newspaper rewrite man did the job. Eye-catching headlines like "A Photograph of Christ" led to short, punchy paragraphs about the "linen cloth of ancient weave," "imprints made by the body of a dead man," and the other compelling shroud facts; each page was illustrated with a photograph or a line drawing. By early 1954, 130,000 pamphlets had been sent out, according to the *Holy Shroud Guild Bulletin,* a mimeographed newssheet which the guild had started mailing out to its membership in June 1952. Active membership was approaching one thousand, with members in thirty-seven of the then forty-eight states.

In 1956, hoping to generate some new finding of his own, Otterbein visited the Eastman Kodak Company in Rochester, New York. The shroud, after all, was a photographic phenomenon of sorts, and he hoped that photographic experts would be able to shed new light on its mysteries. The Kodak executives were cordial, and discussed the problem at a round table; but the best they could offer was a promise of help in planning another photographing session, should the shroud be shown publicly again.

Francis Cardinal Spellman, archbishop of New York, visiting the massive collection of shroud material—books, sculpture, photographs—at Mount St. Alphonsus Redemptorist Seminary, Esopus, New York (HSG)

Several months later Otterbein called on Dr. James Manning, head physicist-chemist at the New York City Police Crime Laboratory in Brooklyn. Without actually seeing the shroud itself, he couldn't say much; however, as Otterbein later wrote, "He suggested a study or analysis of the cloth's weave. We pointed out that this had already been done. . . . Next he suggested the possibility of a chemical analysis to discover the substances which caused the stains. Then we had to point out that it was almost certain that chemical analysis would not be permitted because if the bloodstains were really the blood of Christ, it would not be fitting that this should be subjected to chemical analysis.

"Dr. Manning grasped the reasons which seemed to exclude direct chemical analysis and replied that there were several other possibilities; e.g., X-ray diffraction and microspectroscopy. He then explained both processes and indicated that they might reveal the presence of haemin crystals on the cloth. These microcrystals would make possible definitive identification of the stains as bloodstains. On the other hand, Dr. Manning told us that at least 96 organic substances in human blood have been identified, and as soon as blood is exposed to the air, multiple and rapid changes take place. Hence, positive identification of the blood as blood would not seem possible except by reason of the haemin crystals."

Later that year, Otterbein visited the Federal Bureau of Investigation in Washington, D.C. The result was the same. They suggested how to test the cloth but could say nothing without seeing the cloth itself.

In 1957 Otterbein presented the shroud story on WBZ–TV in Boston. While the show was in progress, a crew from the archdiocese of Boston filmed the program. The resultant twenty-nine-minute film was turned over to Modern Talking Pictures, a distribution company with offices in twenty-eight American cities. Thirty copies of the film were made, and MTP estimates that perhaps as many as 250,000 people—school assemblies, church groups, women's clubs—saw the film before the prints wore out.

But perhaps Otterbein's greatest contribution to the advancement of knowledge about the shroud has to do with encyclopedias.

Herbert Thurston, a British Jesuit, known at the turn of the twentieth century as an objective and searching writer of exceptional knowledge in the fields of history, liturgy, and hagiography, was one of the most influential people in the modern history of the shroud. As a result of his special interests, he would become expert in the occult, eventually writing books on mysticism, ghosts, and poltergeists. But he condemned the authenticity of the shroud in the 1912 edition of the *Catholic Encyclopedia,* and for the next fifty-six years anyone wanting quick and reliable information on it read Thurston's badly misinformed article.

Thurston first attacked the shroud in 1903. In two long articles for *The Month,* a scholarly Catholic publication, he detailed everything that had been said against the shroud in continental Europe. He included the explanation that the shroud images had probably been produced by an accidental inversion of its colors through the centuries—a theory, by the way, that had already been refuted by Vignon. He felt that the fourteenth-century documents proved nothing but that the shroud was a painted fraud and that the absence of historical documentation before that time was proof enough that it was not genuine.

"It appears to me quite conceivable that the figure of our Lord may have been originally painted in two different yellows, a bright glazed yellow for the lights and a brownish yellow for the shadows. What chemist would be bold enough to affirm that under the action of time and intense heat (like the fire of 1354) the two yellows may not have behaved very differently, the bright yellow blackening, the brown yellow fading?"

Having never seen the shroud himself, Thurston had relied heavily on the authority of a French associate, Abbé Ulysse Chevalier, who had never seen the shroud either. Both of these learned gentlemen refused to accept the firsthand report that there was no paint on the shroud.

Some forty-five years later, another Jesuit priest, this time an American, took a different position on the shroud. Having read the first favorable article to appear in a standard Catholic reference work—the 1953 edition of the *Enciclopedia Cattolica*—Walter Abbott reported the findings in the April 1955 issue of the *American Ecclesiastical Review*.

The first part of the article was written by Pietro Scotti, the priest-chemist who took part in the 1950 sindological conference; he noted that providential circumstances had to occur before the stains were produced on the shroud and that the essential circumstance was certainly the resurrection. The second part was written by Alberto Vaccari, a Jesuit priest and Scripture scholar at the Pontifical Biblical Institute in Rome. Vaccari concluded that the Gospel of John was not in conflict with the existence of the shroud, as several Scripture scholars had maintained. Shortly thereafter Walter Abbott himself wrote a heavily pro-shroud article for the supplement mailed to buyers of the English-language *Catholic Encyclopedia*.

It was not until 1968, however, that the Thurston article on the shroud was finally replaced in the encyclopedia by one written by Father Otterbein, who presented an evenly balanced statement of the facts as they stood in the middle of the twentieth century. It included a description of the cloth, various scientific studies that had been carried out with the help of the photographs, and discussions of the historical and scriptural problems. The entry concluded with the following paragraph:

"There are still many unanswered questions, but the accumulation of evidence from different fields of knowledge presents a formidable argument in favor of authenticity. The rapid progress of science and scholarship has made a new exposition of the shroud advisable."

Besides reaching the Catholic reading audience, Otterbein's article had a further impact. In the late 1960s the *Encyclopaedia Britannica* gave a few lines on the existence of the shroud in its periodic updates. When the reference work was totally revised and published in 1974, it contained an article of 120 words:

"Shroud of Turin," read the entry, which was flanked by

a photograph of the face, "linen cloth purporting to be the burial cloth of Christ. . . . In 1898, the first photographic plates were made of it. . . . After studying this evidence two professors of biology presented to the Academie des Sciences in 1902 their conclusions. . . . The history of the shroud, however, cannot be traced beyond the mid-14th century."

The article, of course, was not entirely satisfactory to Otterbein, but at least the world of secular scholarship was beginning to take notice of the existence of the shroud and would presumably have to deal with it in the near future. ∎

Port Chester

ASSISTING Otterbein with the Holy Shroud Guild is Peter M. Rinaldi, S.D.B. At the time of the 1933 exposition he was a Salesian seminarian and acted as interpreter for the many pilgrims and curiosity-seekers who visited Turin that year. The first magazine article of consequence on the shroud published in the United States was written by him; it appeared in the June 1934 issue of the *Sign,* a national Catholic monthly. This was the article that had ignited Fr. Edward Wuenschel's lifelong interest in the shroud. Forty-one years later he would write again for the *Sign.* In the February 1975 issue, in an article entitled "I Saw the Holy Shroud," he gave his impressions of the 1973 exposition.

Through his interest in the shroud, Rinaldi touched another soul, Mrs. I. Sheldon Tilney. When she read Wuenschel's article in the March 1937 *Scientific American,* she became an ardent supporter of the shroud and eventually a convert to Catholicism. Ironical, perhaps, is the fact that her husband was secretary, and her brother president of, *Scientific American.*

"The Tilneys spent their winters in Palm Beach, Florida," Rinaldi recalls. "I was in Tampa at the time she visited me, and I arranged to give a number of lectures on the shroud, several to be at her home. One of those lectures, by the way, was attended by Mrs. Rose Kennedy and some of her children."

In 1940 and again in 1971, Rinaldi arranged for the publication of his own books on the shroud. The one in 1940 was *I Saw the Holy Shroud,* which sold almost 100,000 copies. The book in

Over   **American sindologists Rev. Peter M. Rinaldi, S.D.B., and Rev. Adam J. Otterbein, C.Ss.R, holding the shroud photographically reproduced on linen. This reproduction, along with other sindonalia, are in the "Christ of the Holy Shroud" shrine in Corpus Christi Church, Port Chester, New York. (HSG)**

1971 was *It Is the Lord: A Study of the Shroud of Christ;* sales of the clothbound edition and the subsequent paperback edition will probably equal that of its predecessor.

In 1950, upon becoming pastor of Corpus Christi Church, Port Chester, New York, Rinaldi erected a shrine to the shroud with financial help from Mrs. Tilney. Though considerably smaller than the magnificent chapel housing the shroud in Turin, it was decorated with a marble statue of the body of Jesus, a mural depicting his burial, and a life-size transparency of the shroud's frontal image illuminated from the back. In 1970 the shrine was relocated to the side of the church, enlarged considerably and enriched with mosaics and paintings. A recent addition to the church is a crucifix with a life-size corpus. One of three fashioned by Msgr. Giulio Ricci, it has the more-than-one-hundred flagellation marks that are discernible on the shroud.

In 1963 Random House published *The Shroud* by John Walsh. Unlike most others who had written about the shroud, Walsh was a professional writer, and consequently his book was a highly readable, informative, and objective account of the 1898 events, the 1931 exposition, and its immediate aftermath. In researching the shroud, he had conferred at length with Father Wuenschel and interviewed the surviving relatives of Secondo Pia, Paul Vignon, and Pierre Barbet.

"Only this much is certain," Walsh said in the Preface, "the shroud of Turin is either the most awesome and instructive relic of Jesus Christ in existence—showing us in its dark simplicity how he appeared to men—or it is one of the most ingenious, most unbelievably clever products of the human mind and hand on record. It is one or the other; there is no middle ground."

Another vigorous sindonologist whom I was never to meet but who presented the shroud story to middle America was Francis L. Filas, a Jesuit priest, professor of theology at Loyola University, Chicago.

In 1952 he persuaded executives of WNBQ–TV in Chicago to let him present the shroud story on Good Friday. They agreed. The thirty-minute program ran at noon, and by 5:00 P.M. the station received four hundred telephone calls from viewers asking that the program be repeated. In an era when few people had television sets, this was an overwhelming response. Before the month was out, Filas had received 3,100 letters.

On Good Friday, 1954, the American Broadcasting Company televised the show to thirty of its network stations. Viewers in Illinois, Massachusetts, Florida, Louisiana, Missouri, Michigan, and some of the Rocky Mountain states saw Father Filas, in business suit and Roman collar, spotlight various details on the shroud photographs with a long wooden pointer. "Is the shroud authentic?" was the question Filas asked, and then he gave as much proof as he could. At the program's end, he told viewers that if they wanted more information, they should write to the Holy Shroud Guild, of which he was vice-president. This time he got 13,000 letters.

By 1959 the shroud show was a tradition in the Chicago area. The ABC television network broadcast it to eighty-six different geographical audiences from California to New York, and *Time* magazine described it as one of the outstanding telecasts of the Easter weekend. In 1968 it was estimated that the show had drawn 150,000 pieces of mail. In 1974 Father Filas said that approximately forty-six million viewers had seen the program since it first began. ∎

Miami

I HAD BEEN HOME for about a month, reading and analyzing the material I'd gathered, before I realized that there were many areas that I wanted to explore personally before I started to write.

The anthropology of the shroud images, for example, had been delved into by few researchers—Luigi Gedda and Giulio Ricci were the two names that came to mind. They had gone to great lengths to measure the different parts of the body as delineated in the shroud, but they had said little about what racial character-istics the figure revealed.

To get an objective, impartial analysis of my own, I telephoned

116

the Smithsonian National Museum of Natural Sciences in Washington and asked to speak to an anthropologist.

T. Dale Stewart picked up the phone; he had been director of the museum between 1962 and 1965, and was now anthropologist emeritus.

When I explained to him what I wanted, he said that although he had never heard of the shroud, it did sound interesting. He said also that he would be happy to meet with me, but asked that I first send him some material on the shroud, especially the Enrie photos.

I could see a trip to Washington looming on the horizon. Perhaps I would have to hit the road again.

For further information on the textile aspects of the shroud, I decided to write to the two museums in Lyons, the ones Père Bourguet had suggested I visit to see if I could find among the pieces of the Gayet collection facial or bodily imprints on the burial clothes found at Antinoe, Egypt.

Reading the last chapter of Paul Vignon's 1902 book on the shroud, I came across a startling paragraph.

"M. Gayet has shown me all sorts of shrouds found in Egyptian tombs. In some cases, the mummy has left vague imprints on the enveloping cloth like a brown stain devoid of shape and gradation. I have thought I recognized the print of a back, but no distinct shape was visible. M. Gayet was good enough to give me the Egyptian shroud on which this brown shading was perceptible. Perhaps some day it may serve to prove that there is no resemblance between the mark on this coarse outer casing and the print at Turin, which is equivalent to a portrait. There is no possible resemblance between the stains caused by . . . decomposition and the picture produced [on the shroud]."

So it seems that Vignon had not only met Gayet but had also come to the same conclusion as I—albeit some seventy years before. ■

Another area that I felt had not been sufficiently explored was Jewish burial practices. I telephoned the Jewish Theological

117

Seminary in New York City, explained my problem to the public relations office, and was connected to Dr. Dov Zlotnic, professor of rabbinic literature. Intrigued by my question, but unable to discuss the several possible answers on the telephone, Dr. Zlotnic said that he would see me any time during my next visit to Manhattan.

> The reason I telephoned Jewish Theological was that Fr. Edward Wuenschel had also met with someone there. He was one of the few sindonologists who actually consulted Jewish experts for information on ancient Jewish burial procedures. In the foreword to his book about the shroud, *Self-Portrait of Christ,* he acknowledged "special thanks to Rabbi Jacob Menkes, a noted authority on rabbinical lore." ∎

In searching for the most probable theory of how the images were actually transferred to the cloth, I decided to try the young science of parapsychology, which dealt with strange and unusual phenomena. I telephoned Dr. Karlis Osis, head of the American Society for Psychical Research in New York City.

Osis said he would be glad to see me, but didn't I think that an optical physicist would be the appropriate person to study the shroud photographs? The one he recommended was Dr. John Rush, professor at the University of Colorado, Boulder.

> The reason Osis appealed to me was that he had conducted an interesting study in which he had questioned approximately 640 doctors and nurses who attended deathbed patients. The results were dramatic. A significant number of the medical professionals reported that the dying patients had "an elevated mood" just before their deaths and talked of a kind of otherworld which they seemed to be moving into; they even got angry when some of the doctors tried to revive them. "It's so beautiful there," the moribund had said. ∎

Still another area that I felt needed exploration was photographic analysis. Remembering I had once seen a magazine that mentioned a Kodak man in connection with the shroud, I dug through my mountain of shroud material until I found it: a letter to the editor of the *British Journal of Photography,* dated June 30, 1967.

Walter Clark was the letter-writer's name. He wrote that he was affiliated with Eastman Kodak Company's research laboratories, and that in 1930 or 1931 a Lt. Col. P. W. O'Gorman had come from England to ask him some questions about the shroud image. Clark said he had volunteered a guess: peroxides from the burial spices had caused oxidation of the linen, and this in turn formed an image. Ammonias, in a process called chemical vapography, were known to do this on cellulose, and linen, he pointed out, was cellulose. In other words, as he saw it, the shroud image was the result of the chemical vapography, but through peroxide vapors instead of ammonia vapors, and without a sensitized cloth.

I decided to try a long shot. I called telephone information in Rochester and got a number. Much to my surprise and delight, Clark answered the phone. We talked awhile, but Clark said there wasn't anything he could add to the explanation he'd offered forty years before. The trouble with that explanation, I told him, was that some chemists don't believe vapors will travel in straight lines and thus etch a good image. Clark maintained that they might be able to do so if the atmosphere were still and damp enough.

He added that O'Gorman hadn't liked the chemical explanation either.

The article that O'Gorman wrote on the shroud appeared in the May 1931 issue of *The Catholic Medical Guardian.* He later revised and expanded his theory into a speech which he gave in London; the speech appeared in a 1940 issue of the *American Ecclesiastical Review.*

What O'Gorman came up with was a theory combining the action of four different agents: oxidizing vapors such as those postulated by Vignon; radioactive substances which may have been in the burial spices or even in the body parts themselves; "electrical radiations of an auracal nature;" and "a sudden radiance of our Lord's body at the moment of the resurrection." ■

The best thing for me to do now, Clark suggested, was to contact Charles Bridgeman at the Kodak Marketing Educational Center in Rochester. "He has vast experience in the examination of works of art and in the techniques of radiography, ultraviolet light and infrared photography, and I think he'd be the best one able to pass judgment on the new shroud photos."

I thanked Clark and took his advice. I called Bridgeman, who said he'd be glad to look at the photos and to send them up.

"What an exciting thrill it was to see the photographs of the shroud of Turin" were the first words of Bridgeman's response several weeks later.

"The more one studies these pictures, the clearer it becomes that any evaluation based upon them alone would be of little help unless a thorough scientific examination were undertaken, and this seems out of the question.

"My specific area of investigation involves radiography, and even in this area, I could not state what created a specific image on the film without a chemical analysis of the substance traversed by the X-rays. I hope you can see that any comment I might make would be of no value." ■

Radiation was an intriguing theory, and I decided to telephone the University of Miami Medical School, where I was given the name of Dr. Harold E. Davis, a retired professor of radiology and a fellow of the American College of Radiology.

When I showed him the Enrie photographs, he remarked that they resembled X-rays; beyond that he was unwilling to go. For an expert opinion, he suggested I consult someone else, like E. Dale Trout of the University of Oregon, who, he said, had been one of General Electric's finest radiation physicists.

Trout, when I reached him by phone, suggested that the one to see was Wade Patterson, a radiation physicist at the Lawrence Livermore Laboratory near San Francisco, a facility run by the University of California at Berkeley for the U.S. Atomic Energy Commission.

Patterson said he would be glad to receive me, and we made an appointment.

120

Since it appeared I would be spending some time in the very near future in California, I decided to try to track down Ralph Graeber, "the guy with the shroud show" in Southern California. It turned out, when I finally got him on the phone, that he had not only undergone a sort of religious conversion, but that he was also a nuclear engineer. The profile of him that evolved in the next few days from telephone calls and letters made him as intriguing and as potentially important to the shroud story as Hans Naber and Leonard Cheshire.

After World War II, during which he served as a B-25 pilot, Graeber enrolled at Purdue University.

As a student of engineering, he worked part time on the university's nuclear project, which was the development of a "linear electron accelerator and synchroton," more commonly known as an atom smasher. After graduation he took a job with the U.S. Atomic Energy Commission's Argonne National Laboratory located at Lemont, Illinois; there he helped develop two of the first big "Van Neumann class" scientific computers, the AVIDAC and the ORACLE.

In 1953, partly because of his work on the pioneering science computers, Graeber was asked to join RCA's budding missile project at Cape Canaveral, Florida. RCA's contract called for the processing of missile flight-test data, and Graeber was asked to work with the team building two SEAC-class computers that were to do the job. When ballistic missiles with supersonic thrusts were fired down the Atlantic Testing Range, he was responsible for one of the first "on-line" computers. And he was at Canaveral when the first American satellites went up.

During this time of rich scientific fulfilment, however, Graeber experienced a religious disillusionment. "As a scientist, I gradually began to realize that theologians and ministers didn't know what they were talking about. Time and again they would spew scientific errors from the pulpit till I couldn't stand Sunday-morning church anymore. This understanding coalesced in the late 1950s while I was at Canaveral. Yet, I felt inside that the basic Bible must contain truth, and that the

121

fault therefore lay with its self-appointed interpreters."

So he started looking through "the occult stuff" and found most of it nauseating, except perhaps the writings of Edgar Cayce and Emmanuel Swedenborg, both of whom were psychics, the one twentieth-century American, the other eighteenth-century Swedish.

Then Graeber read *Autobiography of a Yogi,* a 1946 metaphysical work by the Indian spiritual master Paramahansa Yogananda: "I found the autobiography by far the best philosophy-of-life book that I had ever encountered. I was totally captivated by its profound scientific insights. And I was even more impressed that these insights could be used to remove blockages that inhibit man from using his psychic and intuitional powers. But I also was not naive, and I knew that Southern California [where Yogananda's followers, the Self Realization Fellowship, had established its headquarters] was full of kooks. So I prayed very hard to Jesus to tell me if Yogananda's message was the same that Jesus had taught. Then, the very next issue of the *Self-realization* magazine had the shroud face printed on the rear cover, and the instant I saw it I realized fully that it was the answer to my prayer."

The expression on the shroud face was exactly like the expression Graeber had seen so many times on pictures of Yogananda's face, he said, and in many respects like the expression on the face of Yogananda's master, Sri Yukteswar, who died in 1935.

"It is said that a picture is worth ten thousand words," Graeber said, "and to me the similarities were a positive and total indication that both Yogananda and Jesus knew and taught the same things."

Graeber left Canaveral in the early sixties and took a job in Burbank, California, where he could be near the Self-Realization centers. "I still had a great love for Jesus and his teachings, and I considered it pitiful that his millions of followers knew nothing of the true photograph of him and the deep insight into his nature which it conveyed." So, seeing the shroud as a vehicle that might bring about this enlighten-ment, and also seeing that his scientific background was

122

uniquely suited to spread the shroud story, Graeber said that, along with learning from Yogananda, he would become unofficial publicity man for the shroud on the West Coast.

His first project was to assemble a slide show. For pictures, he said, he sent away to the Holy Shroud Guild in Esopus, New York. For specific information he read books by Wuenschel and Barbet. Then he took to the road, showing the slides all over Southern California.

Next Graeber decided to design and sell shroud greeting cards. His first was a simple one: the shroud face on one side; and on the other, a poem he'd written about the relic. The second was more sophisticated; on the front it had one of the beautiful NASA photographs of earth, as seen from outer space, with the word *peace;* on the inside was a picture of the positive shroud face, with considerable text explaining the shroud images on the slides he showed. "The text was very heavy," said Graeber. "It was a mixture of Eastern philosophy and Western science, and the groundswell of interest I had envisioned never developed."

After Graeber and I had talked long distance a couple of times, I began to realize that he felt the images on the shroud had been formed by some kind of radiation from the body and that the radiation had possibly caused heat. "To space-age scientists, it is quite obvious that the images were formed by radiation processes," said a paragraph in the text of his second card. ". . . and the linen was scorched by the Nova," said a line in the poem on the smaller card. ■

Graeber's use of the word *scorched* made me riffle through the notes I made in Turin. In a few moments I found what I was looking for. Yes, Fr. Peter Rinaldi had used the same word to describe the body imprints the day he and I saw the shroud in the Hall of the Swiss.

Graeber's and Rinaldi's use of the word *scorched* reminded me of an article I had read in *Sindon,* the journal of the Cultores Sanctae Sindonis in Turin. It was in a 1966 issue, and its author was British journalist and author, Geoffrey Ashe.

123

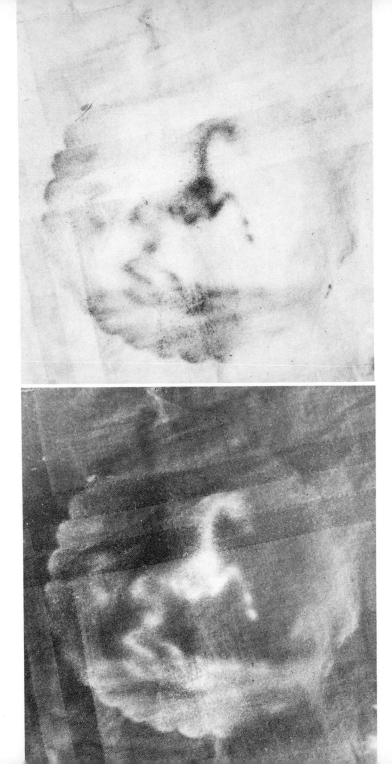

Origin of image:
The scorch theory

In 1966 British sindonologist Geoffrey Ashe heated the horse brass below, pressed it on a linen cloth, and then photographed the scorched image. The positive and negative images are on the opposite page. (GA)

His theory was that the images on the shroud may have been the result of scorching. To test his theory, he took a horse brass, a metal medallion, about three inches in diameter, with a horse in relief in its center. He heated the medallion, placed it relief-side-up on a flat surface, and then laid a handkerchief over it, stretching the handkerchief gently "so as to smooth it out and give as uniform a contact as possible without direct pressure or sagging."

After a few seconds, wrote Ashe, "a brown 'scorch-picture' was visibly forming and coming through to the upper side." He quickly lifted the cloth from the metal, and the result was a negative picture of the horse that was quite detailed. All the parts of the figure that were in direct contact with the handkerchief came out dark; the parts not in direct contact came out lighter or not at all.

"The physical change of the body at the resurrection," concluded Ashe, "may have released a brief and violent burst of some radiation other than heat—perhaps scientifically identifiable, perhaps not—which scorched the cloth. In this case, the shroud is a quasi-photograph of Christ returning to life, produced by a kind of radiance or 'incandescence' partially analogous to heat in its effects. . . . In conclusion, the acceptance of the holy shroud as a 'scorch picture'—whatever the precise mode of creation—justifies the following statement: 'The shroud is explicable [only] if it once enwrapped a human body to which something extraordinary happened. It is not explicable otherwise.' "

The flash-of-heat-and-light theory advanced by O'Gorman in the thirties and Ashe in the sixties seemed to be acquiring a new respectability in the seventies.

"The one thing you must realize," Graeber said to me, "is that man's body is not what it appears to be. This is basic to nuclear science, space-age science, and occult science. The body is a marvelous collection of spinning electrons grouped into cells, and these cells are grouped into nerves, blood, muscle, bone, et cetera. And all the time there is continuous electrical motion in the atoms, and where there is electrical motion there are electromag-

126

netic fields, and electromagnetic fields radiate out. . . . In a nutshell, the radiations are there whether anybody wants to say they are or not. They always have been, and always will be, wherever matter exists."

I knew in a general way what Graeber was talking about. When I was researching parapsychology, I'd come across scientists who, in arguing for the existence of immaterial entities such as a surviving consciousness after death, had pointed out that matter, contrary to what it seems to the human senses, is not, at its essence, material.

They had explained it this way:

All things are made of atoms, and atoms are made of protons, neutrons, electrons, and other atomic particles. But none of these particles are matter in the same way that a table or a chair is. They were described as being made out of "electricity" or "energy." Some parts of the atom actually exhibited the characteristics of "anti-matter," a word coined to express their essential immateriality. They were strange particles, and their very existence meant that there was a basic nonmateriality in all material things.

Einstein's famous formula—energy equals mass times the velocity of light squared—was an expression of this basic immateriality. It stated that material, or mass, was nothing more than converted energy and that energy was nothing but converted mass. But what was energy? Besides naming its various forms— heat, light, electricity, and so forth—no one really knew.

Now, in relation to the shroud, Graeber was expanding my knowledge of nuclear science when he explained that moving electrons—one of the mysterious parts of the atoms—give off radiation. And since all things are made of atoms, it therefore follows that all things give off radiation.

"Man is not the hundred-and-fifty-pound chunk of solid matter portrayed by the very limited five senses," iterated Graeber. "He never was, and never will be. Man is 'in the image of God'— spinning constantly, changing cycles, from the tiniest electrons to the entire body. And the electrons circling their centers are surely 'in the image' of earths circling suns, suns circling galaxies, and galaxies circling what scientists now call the 'big bang' center, which yogis in the ancient Vedas have long called 'Vishnuave.' "

Graeber, much as he appeared to be, wasn't trying to be mystical.

"It is wrong to refer to the radiation that caused the shroud images as extranatural. Its operation is the operation of a natural law that stuffed-shirt Western science simply hasn't gotten around to investigating. . . . The Greeks gave us the concept of the atom thousands of years before the West ever got around to its so-called discovery. The masses consider natural that which is *familiar*—not that which is explained. The human heartbeat is much more extranatural than the shroud image, but it is considered natural only because it is so familiar. And it will probably be a long time before the shroud radiation becomes equally familiar.

"All discovery of new scientific laws starts with a flash of mental insight into the causative elements of a perplexing situation. Then comes the publishing of the new concept; the entrenched-position people then heap fire on the head of the innovator, controversy flourishes, and eventually a majority BECOME AWARE of the new idea, and judge it to be true. Thus the concept becomes a scientific law until a new and better—deeper and more comprehensive—concept comes along. The scientific awareness of radiation only dates back to World War Two.

"And there is also the matter of degrees of explanations to be kept in mind when talking of the shroud images. Nothing is ever fully explained. When a phenomenon is reproducible, that which is enough to satisfy a majority of observers changes constantly. For example, prior to photography the image was explained as a miracle, and this satisfied the masses. So it was considered explained. After photography, there was the vapography, which, for a while, was accepted as the explanation—and it did crudely reproduce the negative phenomenon. Now radiation must be added, and it too will serve for a while. Then other things will be found, and it will be explained again and again—and so on.

"I really don't know if we'll ever be able to fully comprehend what happened in the shroud—at least not until our understandings are raised to the highest level."

Before leaving for Washington, I decided to write to the European sindonologists I'd met to inquire if anyone had consulted a nuclear physicist on the possibility of radiation causing the images on the shroud.

I also sent a letter to the U.S. Department of Commerce's National Technical Information Service and the *Encyclopaedia Britannica*'s research service; any mentions of the images of human corpses being transferred to cloths would be most appreciated, I wrote; and I enclosed checks to cover their fees.

They were sorry, both organizations wrote back, but to their knowledge no such references existed, unless one counts those mentions of the shroud of Turin from the fourteenth century on. ■

Washington

WHEN I ARRIVED at the Smithsonian National Museum of Natural Sciences, I entered the north foyer, where I was greeted by a saber-toothed tiger. The sign said it was a prehistoric beast, but the taxidermist had made it look at though it was about to devour me for its lunch.

I asked for T. Dale Stewart, and I was told he had just gone to lunch.

Once again I had to wait.

While waiting, I decided to reread the conclusion of *The Shroud of Turin* by the German Jesuit Werner Bulst, which had been published in Germany in 1954 and in the United States in 1956.

"Is it possible to determine more closely the nationality of this man on the cloth? Since we have only a frontal image, and moreover, since the color of the skin, hair, and eyes is unknown, it would hardly seem possible to directly determine the racial strain with certitude. Still, the style of wearing the hair and beard allows some deductions. The man was certainly not of the Greco-Roman culture. Of the numerous portraits we have of Greek and Roman origin, there is not one of a man with hair parted in the middle and falling to the shoulders. Likewise, a beard like that on the cloth of Turin is seldom

129

found. Is this in keeping with a Jew in the time of Christ? There was hardly a people in the whole Roman Empire who clung so stubbornly to their customs which, for the most part, were determined by their religious beliefs. It is well known that, in contrast to other peoples, the Jews highly regarded the beard as a manly adornment.

"However, we do not know exactly how men wore their hair in the time of Jesus. But, again in contrast with other peoples even neighboring on Israel, longish hair was thoroughly in keeping with Jewry. In his researches into the Jewish style of wearing the hair, H. Gressman found that they generally wore long hair caught together at the back of the neck. S. Kraus, the distinguished Jewish archaeologist, maintains that both in the talmudic and biblical period to which Gressman extended his study, men wore 'long hair' but 'not too long'— a flexible gauge.

"In any case we can say that the 'portrait' on the cloth of Turin agrees perfectly with what we know from other sources of the Jewish style of wearing the hair. Still these scraps of information are too meager to allow any conclusive proof." ■

Once Stewart arrived back from lunch, we walked down through some of the halls of the institution until we came to his office. I saw the packet of shroud information on his desk, but it turned out that he hadn't had a chance to look at it. He was attentive to my story, however, and when I finished, he made some comments.

"The effect is of a narrow face, characteristic of the caucasoid people—a white man. Orientals tend to be round-faced. Negroes have broad noses and thick lips. That means he could be semitic, but I would have to see the profile to tell for sure. It looks like a large nose, and it might have been quite prominent. But there's no way to be certain without a profile."

If I had known Stewart would need a profile of the man in the shroud, I would have brought along the photographs made by Leo Vala, a photographer of British royalty and a pioneer in the development of the 3-D visual process and cinemascope movie screens. By manipulating light through photo trans-

130

parencies, he produced an image on a normal screen that enabled sculptors to make a three-dimensional model which could then be photographed in profile or indeed from any other angle. In perfecting the process Vala had selected the shroud face as a subject "because it's such a beautiful image."

After publishing the results of his experimentation in the March 8, 1967 issue of *Amateur Photographer,* he became an outspoken critic of anyone who thought the image could have been produced by human hands either through artistry or technology. "I've been involved in the invention of many complicated visual processes, and I can tell you that no one could have faked that image. No one could do it today with all the technology we have. It's a perfect negative. It has a photographic quality that is extremely precise."

The more scholarly *British Journal of Photography* published an article on the cloth soon after and it provoked considerable comment—both pro and con—from its readership. ■

"But this comes so close to the traditional representation of Christ," Stewart went on to say, "that you have a built-in bias to contend with. However, that also raises the question of whether artists could have been following some model."

Vignon's iconography theory is what I thought of instantly, as well as Ian Wilson's and Maurus Green's development of it. The reason why Vignon thought of it in the first place was that he was a painter—and it turned out so, too, was Stewart in his leisure time.

The FBI, said Stewart, frequently asked him to identify the race of a person by bones that agents would bring in. "But we can't go beyond broad racial stocks with so little evidence. We can say, these are from a white man, a Negro, or a Mongoloid. But you really need to see a person in life to be positive. The shroud face is that of a white man. I think we can say that. But whether he was from Palestine or Greece, I don't know. I don't think you can be that specific. You'd be challenged. People would say, 'How do you know? What's your proof?' "

Stewart suggested that I put the question to Carlton S. Coon,

Over, and following pages **In 1966 British fashion photographer Leo Vala, by manipulating light through photo transparencies, produced on a screen made of clay an image which was fashioned into a three-dimensional model capable of being photographed from all angles. (LV)**

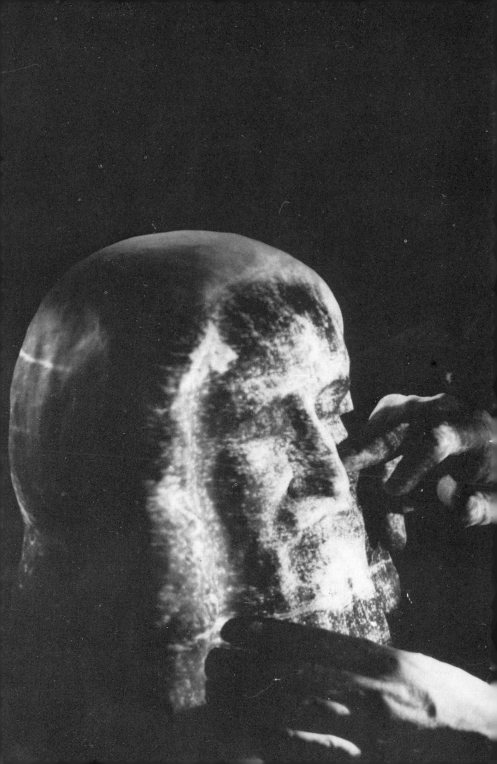

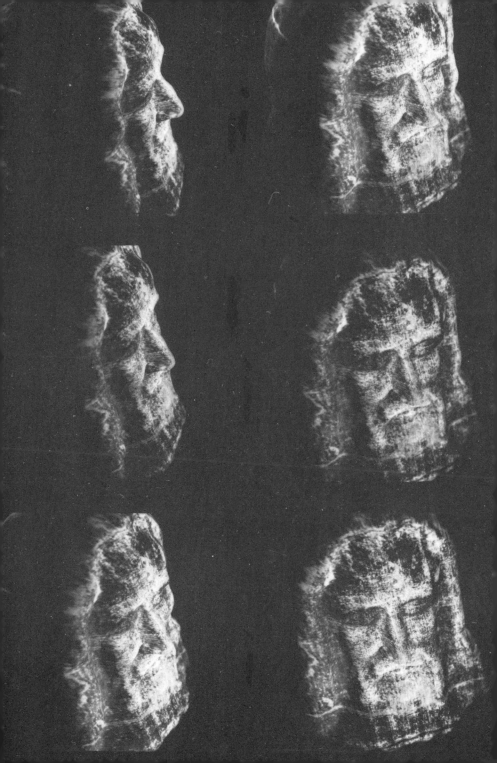

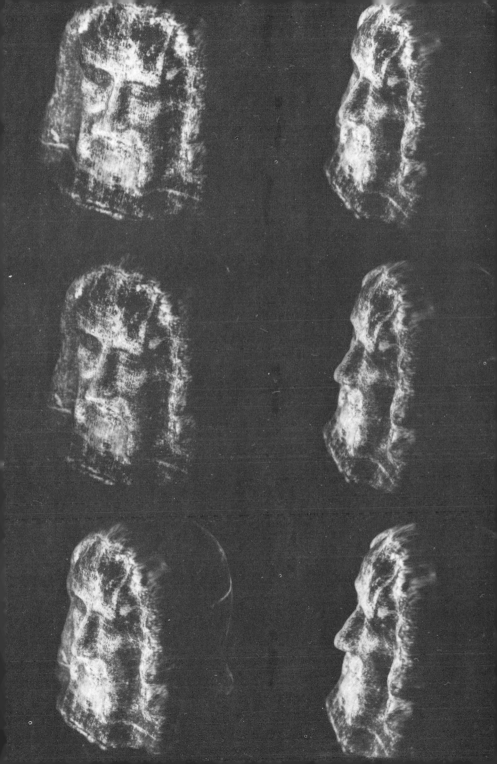

one of the world's most distinguished ethnologists. A former Harvard professor and ethnology curator at the University of Pennsylvania, Coon had written books on the racial classifications of people all over the world. "He'd be the man who might be able to give you some answers."

"Here are the pictures that you asked me to return," Coon wrote back in a week's time.

"Whoever the individual represented may have been, he is of a physical type found in modern times among Sephardic Jews and noble Arabs. The soft parts of the nose have shrunken a bit, which is simply a sign of death. I have seen the same thing in the mummies of Egyptian pharaohs.

"For what it is worth, that is my opinion."

Coon's opinion was worth a great deal, especially in view of the fact that he had traveled widely throughout the Middle East, Asia, South America, and Africa. He was also the author of fifteen books in the area of anthropology, including *The Origin of Races,* published in 1962; and *The Living Races of Man,* published in 1965. As if these weren't enough accreditation, he is credited with the discovery of at least one ancient-man fossil, Arterian man, and with leading the expeditions that discovered two others: Hotu man and Jebel Ighoud man No. 2. ■

My next stop in Washington was the Textile Museum on S. Street, where I hoped to show the shroud photographs to a staff expert.

When I was doing my first set of articles on the shroud in 1971, I had called the museum from Miami to find out if linen cloth could have survived two thousand years.

Anthony Landreau, the acting director at that time, said there was no doubt that it could. "We have fragments of linen preserved from ten thousand B.C.," he said. ■

Arriving at the museum's reception room, I was referred to a young woman assistant; when I told her what I wanted, she

136

looked most skeptical indeed. She said there was no one available at the moment, but if I wanted to leave the photographs with a note, she would see to it that they reached someone who knew about such things; nothing, however, could be done that day. She probably thought I was some kind of religious fanatic. As I headed for the door, I knew I would not be hearing from the Textile Museum any time in the near future.

> Some time later Louise Mackie, associate curator of the
> Textile Museum, told me over the phone that she didn't believe
> any conclusive statements could be made about the shroud
> on the basis of photographs alone. "Seeing and handling make
> a difference," she said. "However, it appears to be a very
> basic weave. Maybe someone with experience in Middle
> Eastern fabrics could tell you more." She suggested a curator
> at the Metropolitan Museum in New York. ∎

Tracking down the possibility that the shroud images might be related to the shadows formed at the time the atom bomb was dropped on Hiroshima, I visited the Atomic Energy Commission's library. There I located several books, one of which was a 1972 work entitled *The Day Man Lost*. Authorship was ascribed to a group called the Pacific War Research Society, and the publisher was Kodansha International, Ltd., of Tokyo, Japan, and Palo Alto, California. Photographs of some of the shadows were included in the book. One showed the shadow of a ladder that had once been permanently attached to a watertank; another, the rough silhouette of a man who had been sitting on stone steps. But the book was not clear as to exactly how the shadows or silhouettes had been formed. On returning to the hotel, I wrote for more information to the Hiroshima Peace Memorial Museum.

> "We received your letter inquiring about shadows formed
> at the time of the A-bomb blast in our city," wrote back
> Kazuharu Hamasaki, curator of the Hiroshima Peace Memorial
> Museum.
> "Frankly speaking, we have no definite idea whether the
> shadows were formed only by heat rays or gamma rays, or by

137

both heat rays and gamma rays. But here in Hiroshima it is widely believed that the shadows were made by enormous heat rays burning or melting everything. And when the heat rays were blocked by objects in their path, unburned areas were made right behind the objects as shadows of them." ∎

Since the shroud was the bloody remnant of an execution, I decided to try a long shot. I telephoned the FBI and asked if someone in their crime lab could look at the Enrie photographs and attempt an analysis of the causes of death.

I was told to send the material and to await a response that would definitely be forthcoming.

Which is what I did.

"Our normal policy," replied Clarence M. Kelley, newly appointed director of the FBI, "requires that the FBI laboratory conduct examinations of evidence in criminal cases for all duly constituted law enforcement agencies. Although exceptions to this policy are possible, it has been found that examinations of the type you requested from photographs are not productive. Examination of the original material would be a more appropriate procedure; however, since such material is in custody of another country, it is not within the province of this Bureau to conduct such examinations." ∎

San Diego

MY FIRST STOP in California was San Diego, the new home of Dr. Robert Bucklin, the midwestern clinical pathologist who had written an article on the shroud which appeared in the January 1970 issue of *Medicine, Science, and the Law,* a journal of the British Academy of Sciences. He helped me in some of the medical areas pertaining to the relic, including making a determination about Hans Naber's several theories; he didn't think they were accurate.

Los Angeles

THE NEXT DAY I flew to Los Angeles. Graeber's voice on the telephone suggested a suntanned, robust, military-looking technician often seen in NASA photographs. I was surprised, then, when a tall, thin, conservatively dressed man of about fifty walked forward and introduced himself as Ralph Graeber.

He told me, that after a series of personal and financial troubles, two good things happened. He had gotten together many of his ideas on modern science and religion, and he was offered a job on the research staff of Systems Development Corporation, a division of the Rand Corporation, the think-tank company used frequently by the American government.

With the help of the sophisticated computers at SDC, he hoped to initiate a new shroud project: restoration of the shroud images to an almost flawless state by using "space-age image-correction techniques." These techniques had been developed by NASA's Jet Propulsion Lab to correct lens distortion and other "noise" in photographs taken by unmanned space probes. The result would be a sharper, more detailed shroud face.

Once settled into a lane on the freeway, Graeber began responding to my questions about the probable origin of the images on the shroud.

It was obvious to any space-age scientist, he said, that the images could have been produced only by some kind of wavelength radiation, by what might commonly be called rays. Vapors don't travel in straight lines, but radiation does. He didn't know precisely what kind of radiation it was, but he felt sure that it was the same kind involved in the formation of the Volckringer leaves.

Rummaging through old herbals and plant books with specimens pressed inside, Dr. Jean Volckringer, chief apothecary at St. Joseph's Hospital, Paris, noticed that sometimes a nearly identical image of a leaf would be formed several pages away from the one on which it was mounted. Somehow the specimen had projected or radiated its image through the pages covering it and onto a blank page beyond.

139

The resulting image was not only sharp—as photographs of them testify—but they were also negatives. They were approximately the same color as the shroud stains—brown—and they even appeared to fade imperceptibly as the shroud stains clearly do. These images were "like a design in sepia," Volckringer was quoted as saying in *Doctor at Calvary.*

"None of these images were to be found in recent herbals," remarked Pierre Barbet, the Paris surgeon who described his work on the shroud in *Doctor at Calvary.* "They were, for instance, very clear in a herbal of 1836, while there were scarcely any markings in a herbal of 1908, which at the time [when Volckringer discovered them] made them 34 years old."

If it had taken a century for the herbal images to project or radiate their images, it is no wonder that sindonologists did not consider radiation a possible explanation for the images on the shroud; after all, as the absence of decomposition stains indicates, the man had been in the shroud for only a few short hours. ■

In the same breath with Volckringer leaves, Graeber mentioned Kirlian photography as a type of radiation possibly involved in the formation of images on the shroud.

In 1939 Semyon Kirlian, a Soviet electrician, while observing a demonstration of a high-frequency machine being used in electrotherapy, noticed a tiny flash of light between the electrodes attached to the patient and the patient's skin. Curious, he wondered if he could photograph it, and accordingly he built himself a high-frequency machine at home. He created a high-frequency electronic field between an electrode from the machine and a metal plate, inserted a piece of film between the two, and placed his hand on the film. Though Kirlian got a severe burn for his efforts, he also got a brilliant photograph of his hand, with a luminescence, or halo, or aura, along the contours of the fingers.

After refining his machine he began photographing all sorts of objects, dead and alive—things such as leaves, coins, and fingers. Eventually, with still further refinements, he was

140

able to photograph entire human bodies without the intermediary of film. And always the results were the same: a glowing luminescence that seemed to radiate from the subject in a myriad of hues—red, blue, green, yellow, and white—rising, fluctuating, churning.

"Around the edges of a leaf," wrote Sheila Ostrander and Lynn Schroeder in *Psychic Discoveries Behind the Iron Curtain,* "there were turquoise and reddish-yellow patterns of flares coming out of specific channels. . . . A human finger placed in the high-frequency field . . . showed up like a complex topographical map. There were lines, points, craters of lights, and flares. Some parts of the finger looked like a carved jack-o'-lantern with a glowing light inside. . . . [The hand] looked like the Milky Way in a starry sky. . . . Multicolored flares lit up, then sparks, twinkles, flashes. Some lights glowed steadily like Roman candles; others flashed out, then dimmed. Still others sparked at intervals."

But what was the luminescence? What was Kirlian seeing? No one knew for sure, wrote Ostrander and Schroeder, but after years of observation Soviet scientists called it "bio-radiation" or an "energy-body" that somehow was inside and emanated from all things.

In living things the emanations appeared to be connected with health. When the aura looked dim and without much vibrance, the person being photographed was found to be either already sick or on his or her way to becoming sick. When it looked strong and brilliant, the person was well and feeling good. The aura wasn't restricted to physical health alone. Anger, hate, tenderness, and joy showed up markedly in the photographs and through the viewing machine. An angry person's aura, for example, turned bright red; blue was a sign of tranquility.

In dead things, the aura seemed to be the slowly diminishing "essence of life." But since completely lifeless things such as coins also had a luminescence, some scientists were moved to speculate that this was the "skeleton" of what once had life. Unlike the "energy-body" of live things, the luminescence of metals was pure white, completely colorless.

141

One of the most surprising finds, according to the American researchers, was that when the Soviet scientists cut part of a subject away—for instance, part of a leaf—they would still get an aura from the section that was missing and in exactly the same shape as the missing part. In other words, the "energy-body" still showed where the material body had been cut off.

Is this the reason why amputees sometimes say that they still feel their severed limb or have sensations in that limb? Ostrander and Schroeder didn't conclude one way or the other, but it was obvious from their account of Kirlian photography that the human body had been discovered emitting radiation. ■

The only difference, Graeber said as we continued along the freeway, between the Volckringer leaves and the Kirlian images was a matter of degree. "The more evolved the matter—from mineral to vegetable, to animal, to man, to saint, and so on—the greater the amplitude of radiation. So great saints, or those of the 'I-am' consciousness, are surrounded by powerful auras, or halos.

"Jesus and saints of all religions have always been portrayed with halos around them. The reason for this is that their radiations were so intense that they could be seen with the naked eye. The Volckringer leaves, however, gave off such low-intensity radiation that it was—what was it?—a hundred years, I believe, after the herbals had been on the shelves before anyone discovered the images."

"But why," it seemed a natural question to ask, "had Jesus' radiation been strong enough to make marks on the cloth when none of the other bodies that had been put in shrouds ever had?"

"Kirlian photography shows that both mental and physical stress increases the loss of life-energy from the body. Now Jesus suffered both extreme mental anguish and extreme physical torture—as much as any man I've ever heard of—before his death. Thus, the intensity level of radiation from his body would have been very great in the tomb."

Besides, Jesus was the embodiment of the highest consciousness there is, said Graeber; the "Son of God" consciousness. Therefore his aura was stronger than any other.

142

There was still another reason why the images in the herbals resembled the shroud images so much. Both the linen of the shroud and the high-grade paper on which the herbals were presumably printed were made of the same vegetable compound, cellulose. Consequently, the Volckringer-Kirlian radiation would have produced approximately the same softly diffused brown stain on the molecular structures of the cellulose material.

The crucial differences between the two types of radiation are in the variables of intensity, exposure duration, and possibly development time. "The Volckringer images were produced by a low-intensity exposure over a long period of time, and the shroud images were produced by a high-intensity exposure over a short period of time. And we don't really know what the development times of either were."

To further prove that a little-known radiation emanates from the body, Graeber gave me the address of a San Francisco man who, he said, was able to see auras with the naked eye. And Graeber promised to give me a copy of a parapsychological classic entitled *The Aura* by J. W. Kilner, a late nineteenth-century physician at St. Thomas's Hospital, London. Kilner, aware of the claims of persons who said they could see the aura with the unaided eye, invented an optical device through which he said he could see the aura himself.

American researchers, notably Thelma Moss and Kendall Johnson of the University of California at Los Angeles (UCLA), confirmed much of what the Soviet scientists had found out about the Kirlian process, which is perhaps better known now as radiation field photography, and eventually added data of their own.

One of the Moss-Johnson tests was to photograph the aura of a person claiming to be a healer. "Energy" that flows out of the healer's body into the body of the patient is often the explanation healers give of the phenomenon that apparently takes place. Energy is also the mode through which acupuncture is said to work; the needles channel the "healing energy" that is said to be circulating through the body into the areas suffering affliction.

The results of the Moss-Johnson tests, as reported in the

After dinner at a vegetarian restaurant in Hollywood, during which we didn't talk at all about the shroud, Graeber invited me to see the observatory in Griffith Park, a forest preserve high in the Hollywood hills, overlooking all of the city and the Pacific Ocean beyond.

I asked him to speculate on exactly what kind of radiation the Volckringer-Kirlian radiation might be.

"Anything I say in this area would be unprovable in terms of volumes of formalized proofs," he said reluctantly. "But I suspect it is somewhere in the ultraviolet region of electromagnetic radiation."

Ultraviolet radiation was close to visible light, I knew, and there it would be a good candidate for what "sensitives" were perceiving when they reported seeing the human aura. Ultraviolet rays could burn, given enough intensity, and therefore they could have caused the scorched look that the shroud images seem to have.

Graeber didn't like my characterizing the shroud images as "scorched." He'd come to prefer to say that the mysterious radiation had acted on the shroud in a manner somewhat analogous to heat but without heat's harshness; perhaps more like light on a photographic plate.

Before I left Los Angeles, Graeber and I would see each other several more times and we would cover the same ground again. Eventually he would send me a copy of *The Kirlian Aura,* a paperback published by Doubleday Anchor Books in 1974. Thinking about him as I often did, I decided that he was an exemplary member of a growing number of scientists who were moving away from hardcore materialism.

For the past 50,000 years all living things have absorbed just about the same amount of Carbon 14, an atom that originates in the atmosphere and then is absorbed by plants and animals. Once the plant or animal dies, this fixed amount of Carbon 14 begins to disintegrate at a fixed rate, which is approximately 50 percent of itself every 5,730 years. In other words, every 5,730 years the amount of Carbon 14 in the remains of the dead plant or animal is approximately half of what it was 5,730 years before. With the aid of large chemistry machines called counters, scientists such as Dr. Willard Libby, of UCLA, can now determine the amount of Carbon 14 left in an object and then compute the object's age. By taking two pieces of the linen that was wrapped around the Dead Sea Scrolls—each piece weighing no more than one-fifth of an ounce—Libby was able to date the scrolls with an accuracy of plus-or-minus fifty years. ■

My next stop was at UCLA to show the shroud photographs to Dr. Willard Libby, a chemist who had won all sorts of honors and prizes—including a Nobel Prize—for his work in organic and nuclear chemistry.

I outlined the history of the shroud as quickly as I could and then showed him the color photographs. He said he knew something about the shroud—it seems someone had once approached him about the possibility of carbon-dating it. He said he was, and still is, interested in doing so, but nothing as yet has come of it.

When I asked who had approached him, he said he had promised not to reveal the name. Needless to say, this reminded me of the secrecy oaths the Turin authorities had forced on the members of the secret 1969 commission.

On the basis of what he knew so far, Libby said he favored a chemical explanation for the origin of the images. It was just a hunch, but he didn't think the images had been produced by radiation unless the radiation were heat waves; but he didn't see how the body, even when alive, could have produced enough heat to cause an image. That would mean postulating some kind of extra-natural heat—and such a phenomenon would take the whole affair out of the realm of science.

When I mentioned Kirlian photography, he replied that one has to be careful in the field of bio-radiation; it's a new field, and there's much in it that is still speculation.

According to the principles of Kirlian photography, a human hand can emit enough radiation to form on a film negative an image like the ones on the following pages. (KJ)

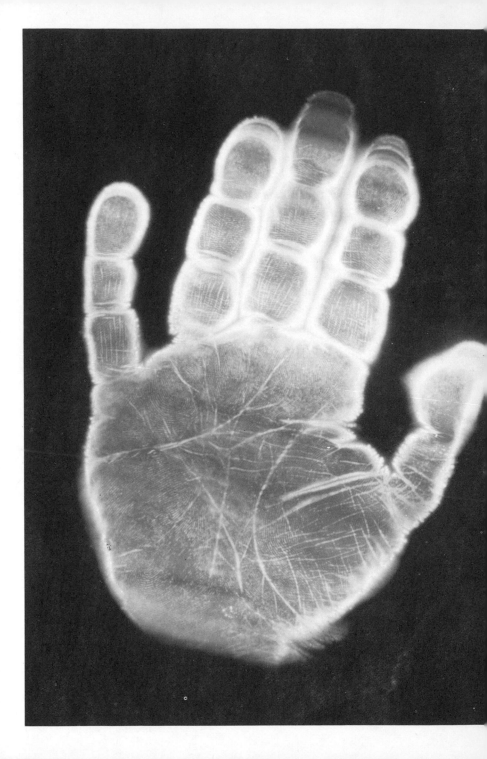

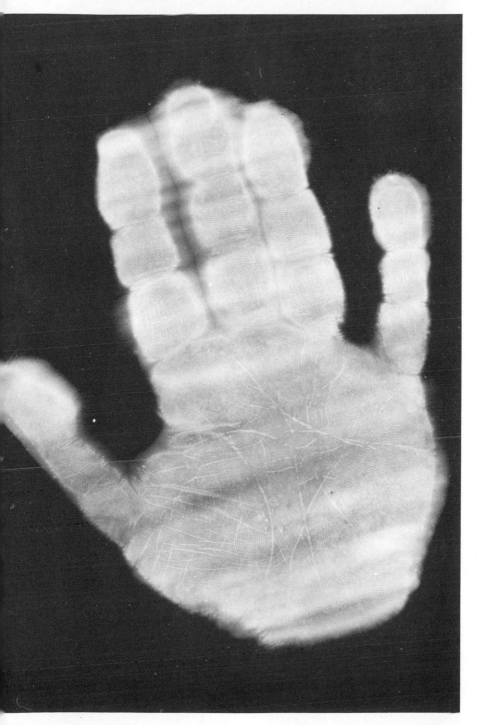

Before I left, Libby suggested I go down to the basement of his building and observe the equipment with which the Carbon 14 test is administered.

> No more than one-sixth of an ounce of the shroud would be consumed if the Turin sindonologists used the latest Carbon 14 dating methods developed by Walter C. McCrone Associates, Inc., of Chicago, Illinois.
> The McCrone Lab is the independent organization that recently analyzed the "Vinland Map" for Yale University and found the early fifteenth-century map of America to be a fake. It had been etched with pigment not invented until the twentieth century.
> The lab's proposal for dating the shroud by the Carbon 14 method has been submitted; the cost would be $12,500, an amount that American sindonologists are more than willing to subsidize. So far, there's not been a word from Turin. ■

Kendall Johnson, forty-five, told me he had become interested in Kirlian photography in 1971 while taking a course under Dr. Thelma Moss, who had heard of the phenomenon during a visit to Russia and introduced it to her class. Johnson subsequently devised a machine to take Kirlian photographs and showed it to his teacher. A partnership developed, experiments were conducted, and the results, once recorded, made them leaders in the field.

He and I were sitting in a UCLA cafeteria examining the shroud photographs; we had just come from the Kirlian Lab set up in the Neuropsychiatric Institute where Dr. Moss had her office.

"There definitely is a similarity here," he said. "The areas of the body that were closest to the shroud show up the darkest, and the areas further away are lighter."

"This is the negative effect I was telling you about," I said.

"Yes," said Johnson, "even to the point of not showing up at all on the parts that were especially far away."

"You mean, the really deep recesses?"

148

"Yes."

Johnson also noticed something that, so far as I knew, no other shroud researcher had ever reported seeing: faintly visible lines traveling down the entire shroud length. They were clearest down the frontal image and in the center of the images, as in an axis that included the nose, the depression between the two pectoral muscles, the hand with the bloodiest wrist, and the groove between the thighs and the calves. The more we looked, the more lines we found; the entire length of the cloth was striated with them.

"We have this too in our photos," said Johnson. "It seems to have something to do with the structure of a nearby object like, perhaps, the table upon which the object being photographed is placed. But we're not sure."

Johnson may have seen similarities in the shroud photos and the Kirlian photos, but he didn't say they both had been made by the same thing. In fact, he stressed that he didn't even know exactly how the Kirlian photos were made. "All we know is that we are getting a picture of an unseen structure. This structure is photographed when electrons sense each other's presence and interact."

The interaction could be captured in the sensitive surface of a film or, indeed, on some other surface that was not photosensitive. the same as when you generate a spark of electricity by walking across a rug and then touch a door knob," he said. "With the right conditions—moisture in the tomb and the unique circumstances of the burial, ointments and such—you might have had an electrical field generated between the slab he was lying on and the air above the body. Then an image might have formed on the cloth. . . ."

Neither he nor I took this speculation seriously for several very obvious reasons. And he thought it extremely doubtful that the shroud images had been formed in exactly the same manner in which Kirlian photographs are made. Perhaps, as Graeber believed, the same radiating "energy" had been at work in both phenomena, but Johnson refused to speculate on that.

My next stop was San Francisco. Johnson volunteered to drive me to the airport. On the way he told me about the book he was writing on Kirlian photography and about how he was supporting himself at the moment by working as an insurance adjuster.

Kirlian photography was the subject of the cover story of the January/February 1974 issue of *The Sciences,* the journal of the New York Academy of Sciences. It focused on the very real possibility that Kirlian photography would be as important a tool in preventive and diagnostic medicine as the discovery of X-rays and the invention of the electroencephalogram. ■

San Francisco

AFTER I got off the plane in San Francisco, I rented a car and headed through the green and purple hills of northwestern Alameda County to the flatter country around Livermore, where the Lawrence Livermore Laboratory was located. An abandoned naval air station in 1950, the complex had been taken over by the U.S. Atomic Energy Commission to found a lab for the production of fissionable material for the development of the first hydrogen bombs, and since that time it has grown to a huge 640-acre, 5,400-employee operation that has developed the Polaris, Poseidon, and Minuteman missiles. Beginning in the Sixties it branched out into peacetime nuclear projects, such as research in nuclear and environmental studies.

Wade Patterson and David S. Myers met me at the reception center, and we walked to a small conference room in the building. Patterson and Myers said that there was a lot of potentially dangerous radiation at Lawrence and that their job was to make sure no one got hurt; they devised and instituted safety measures and monitored levels of radiation absorbed by scientists and their staffs.

Neither of the physicists had ever heard of the shroud before my telephone call a few weeks ago. I gave them a brief rundown on the story and showed them the photographs.

No, they said, they didn't see any way that the shroud images could have been produced naturally by ionizing or high-energy radiation, nuclear or otherwise. X-rays and gamma rays are

150

among the principal ionizing rays, and the images couldn't have been produced by either of them because it takes high-voltage machines to generate X-rays and the only natural sources of gamma rays are radioactive substances like uranium; besides, X-rays and gamma rays don't act on matter in the ways shown on the shroud.

X-rays and gamma rays, they continued, are among the most penetrating radiations; they would have gone right through the shroud instead of marking it. A very intense source of ionizing radiation, they admitted, would have been able to affect the cloth but, given the factors involved—a body, the passage of centuries, and so on—they didn't see how that could have been possible.

Even if by some unlikely chance the body had been made radioactive and was therefore emanating X-rays or gamma rays, the images on the shroud were still not in accordance with the kinds of images that should have formed under these circumstances. X-rays and gamma rays are more strongly absorbed by the bones, said Patterson, and thus bones, and not skin, would have been the most distinguishable aspects of the images.

Even if a radioactive substance such as uranium—which emits gamma rays and alpha and beta particles, all of which are ionizing radiations—had been smeared on the body, the scientists still didn't think the shroud images would have appeared; at best there would have been a silhouette.

If a radioactive substance had been applied in such a way as to emphasize only highlights, they added, they still didn't know of any technique for sensitizing cloth so that it would be able to register high-energy radiation. X-rays were an example of what they meant; film is needed to record the presence of X-rays.

If an atomic blast had gone off over Jerusalem at the time of the burial, there would have been enough high-energy radiation to etch the images on the shroud, but it would have destroyed the shroud itself with its intensity. Even if it didn't destroy the shroud, it would have affected the linen of the shroud in a quite different way.

So much for high-energy, ionizing radiation. But what about low-energy, non-ionizing radiations such as visible light, infrared and ultraviolet radiations? It was conceivable, they were forced to admit, that intense sources of low-energy radiation could have produced the shroud marks by the sheer disposition of heat. But this would be an entirely unnatural situation, since the human body is not known to generate such heat; and since their expertise was not in this area, they did not wish to speculate further on it.

As a parting comment, they suggested that I see a photographic expert at Eastman Kodak in Rochester, New York.

Having a little time to kill before my flight from San Francisco to Denver, I tried to find the American representative of the Assyrian Church, supposedly the oldest Christian Church in the world. The young priest who answered the door said that the prelate had moved and left no forwarding address. He also said that he knew little about the Church's ancient history. ■

Denver / Boulder

WHEN I landed at the Denver airport, I rented a car and drove to Boulder, thirty miles away. It was winter, and the snow-covered peaks of the Rockies could be seen the entire way.

I sat down in the living room of a small ranch house, in front of a picture window facing the Rockies, and showed the shroud photographs to Dr. John Rush, an optical physicist, a scientist with the National Center for Atmospheric Research at the University of Colorado, and a consultant for the Psychical Research Foundation.

After studying the pictures for a while, Rush said, "You need the cloth, and tests. The thing that gets me, however, is the negative image. It's so good. It has remarkable fidelity."

I explained to him the vapograph theory—Vignon's chemical explanation of how the images had formed—and Rush said he was inclined to believe that the images had somehow been formed by chemicals. But he couldn't accept the idea of vapors traveling in straight lines to shape the subtleties of the image, and he was not impressed with the idea that the marks had been scorched into the linen. Ultimately, he admitted he couldn't make any definite remarks about the shroud.

152

When I told him that the Turin authorities had recently conducted secret tests on the shroud, he looked skeptical. "That's like the tobacco companies investigating smoking," he said. "They have too much of a vested interest to be credible." Modern secular science, he added, could do a great deal toward determining the authenticity of the cloth. He suggested that I see a photo expert in Tuscon, Arizona.

Boston

BOSTON was buried in snow when my plane arrived. Fortunately, I had arranged to be met by Richard Orareo, a thirty-five-year-old high school psychologist. I had come across Orareo's name when I was first doing the newspaper series about the shroud in 1971, and we had kept in touch ever since. Not only did he have an excellent knowledge of the shroud story, but he also owned one of the largest shroud libraries in America, second only, it seemed, to the Wuenschel Collection at Esopus, New York.

Orareo had bought the library from the estate of Herman J. Doepner, a fingerprint expert with whom he had been in correspondence for several years. Doepner had died in August 1971 without realizing his life's dream: publication of a manuscript based on years of research in "identology," a field which he believed provided incontrovertible proof of the authenticity of the shroud.

> I hadn't realized the extent of Doepner's involvement with the shroud until I received a letter from his sister, a nun in a St. Paul, Minnesota, convent.
>
> Every morning he arose, said a list of prayers devoted to the shroud, and then spent the rest of the day pouring over life-size blowups of the shroud figures he had mail-ordered from London. "He even had an oil painting of Christ hanging in his bedroom," his sister wrote, "which he loved so much that he told my niece he placed it on the wall which received the morning light so that his first glance upon rising would fall upon the picture."
>
> Doepner never married, and he lived alone in a country

153

cabin somewhere on the outskirts of St. Paul. For a good part of his young-adult and middle-age years he had researched titles for two St. Paul insurance and real estate firms. In 1926 he became interested in fingerprinting, took it up as a hobby, and by the time of his death had assembled a twelve-hundred-volume fingerprint library, which he donated to the International Association of Identification.

Doepner first heard of the shroud in 1952, and in 1956 he retired to devote full time to its study. "Seeing 'identology' as a discipline uniquely suited to study the various marks on the shroud," wrote his sister, "he decided to undertake a scientific study of it. . . . He would prove its authenticity. . . . To do this, he spent eighteen years studying the markings . . . purchased every book and photograph of the shroud available . . . gathered magazine and newspaper articles . . . allowed no one and nothing to interfere. . . . He spared no time, effort, or money. ■

Orareo showed me entire books that Doepner had painstakingly copied, typing page after page, because he could not get anything but a library-loan copy for himself and because he needed them for his study of the shroud.

Precisely what, if anything, Doepner had come up with I couldn't say. I read his manuscript once, hastily, and found one very intriguing hypothesis. He said that, contrary to all previous conceptions, Jesus' body had been laid face down in the tomb, not face up. This explained why the frontal image, and especially the face, was the better etched of the two images on the cloth. Somehow pressure, as it is understood in fingerprinting, had been involved—or so he thought.

Orareo was as helpful as he could be. He spent an entire evening digging through his hall closet, bringing out books and articles I thought I might need for my research. When I was ready to leave, I had fifty pounds of written material crammed into various parts of my luggage, all of it Doepner's. And all of it, I felt sure, would prove immensely valuable when I finally sat down to write my book on the shroud.

Brookline

THE NEXT DAY I had an appointment with Dr. Constantine Cavarnos, a lecturer on Byzantine icons at the Greek Orthodox Theological School, Brookline, Massachusetts. Archbishop Iakovos, head of the Greek Orthodox Church in North and South America, had recommended Cavarnos, a layman, as an expert on Eastern Orthodox history.

Cavarnos told me about the Edessan legends—the same ones that Wilson and Green were working on in England—but said he was sorry, he didn't see how they were related to the shroud. So far as he knew, the Edessan Image had only a face on it, not an entire body like the shroud.

Edward Wuenschel was one of the few sindonologists who had taken the trouble to consult Jewish experts for information on ancient Jewish burial procedures. The results appeared in his book *Self-Portrait of Christ.*

"To determine what was actually done at the burial of Christ, one must read the whole story as related by the four Evangelists." Matthew, Mark, and Luke gave no indication that the body was washed and wrapped as a mummy; John said that the body was wound in linen cloths in the manner of the Jews, which some Scripture scholars interpret as full ritual washing and mummy wrap. But John's description of what happened can be construed in just the opposite way.

"It is reasonable to assume . . . that the jaw was kept in place by a cloth tied under the chin and over the top of the head—an immemorial practice among all peoples. Many commentators believe that this is what John—in chapter 20, verse 7—means when he refers to 'the napkin which was upon his head.'

"It is reasonable to assume also that Joseph, being a wealthy man and wishing to give Christ a decent burial, brought other linens besides the shroud, intending to use these for swathing the body. Not having time to use them for this purpose, he would naturally leave them in the tomb until after the Sabbath, and we may assume that he placed them beside the body, in rolls or bundles. Thus the body would be 'enclosed' in linen cloths—surrounded by the unused swathing bands and enveloped in the shroud—while the head was bound with the jaw-support. The language of John can surely mean this, and it fits in with the rest of the story." ∎

New York City

JEWISH BURIAL CUSTOMS was one of the areas skimpily treated by sindonologists over the years. That was why I had arranged to interview Dr. Dov Zlotnic, professor of rabbinic literature at Manhattan's Jewish Theological Seminary, where the Judaism taught is of the conservative variety. Zlotnic greeted me cordially and bade me sit down. The shelves of books lining the walls made his rather small office look definitely smaller.

I would have preferred to begin simply by asking questions about Jewish burial customs without revealing why I was doing so. However, since I was dealing with a subject that might eventually lead to a discussion of resurrection, I decided to tell him the shroud story first and to show him the photographs.

Zlotnic listened attentively and then proposed two solutions. First, couldn't it be an ancient painting that had lost all extraneous paint matter but still retained some coloring? No, I said, and I gave him the reasons why.

Then couldn't it be the result of sun shining through a stained-glass window for a long time? Before I could say No, he retracted the suggestion, agreeing that it couldn't be so for the reasons already given against the painting theory.

With regard to the ancient burial customs, said Zlotnic, he saw nothing in my description of the shroud that disagreed with them. In order to make any sort of official statement, however, he would have to study the question more thoroughly, something which he couldn't plan to do anytime in the foreseeable future. In the meantime, he said he would have some Xeroxes made of pertinent paragraphs in the seminary library. He also recommended several books on the subject, his own, *The Tractate Mourning,* among them.

156

Zlotnic then took me to lunch in the seminary cafeteria, where we continued to talk about religion in general. When I asked him if he had ever come across shrouds or burial garments with corpse imprints on them, he answered straightway, "I know of no burial cloths that have on them any imprint produced by the body. Shrouds will waste away in the course of time, so there can be no hard evidence from antiquity, except where a preservative agent is used."

The only significant piece of hard evidence concerning Jewish burial practices came into my hands after my interview with Zlotnic.

In the March 18, 1960 issue of the *Catholic Herald,* the British sindonologist Vera Barclay pointed out that at the site of the Qumran Community, which flourished from the second century B.C. to A.D. 70, graves had been uncovered to reveal skeletons in the exact position of the man in the shroud: stretched out flat, face up, and with elbows protruding because of the way the hands had been folded over the pelvic region.

"The significance of the skeletons discovered at Khirbet Qumran in 1951 is that we now have definite confirmation that at the time of Christ some Jews did bury their dead in the actual position of the shroud images. Note [in the picture] that the elbows projecting [out] would not have been convenient for the close winding of the Egyptian way." ■

James Carpenter, professor at General Theological Seminary, confirmed my idea that very little was known about crucifixion.

"Reading the encyclopedias, you'll get about as much knowledge as we have," he said.

I had gotten his name from the *Encyclopedia Americana,* in which he'd written the article on crucifixion.

Bulldozing a hill overlooking Jerusalem in 1968, Israeli construction crews uncovered the tombs of about thirty-five people who had lived around the time of Jesus. One of them, a young man about twenty-five, had been crucified; a seven-inch nail was still stuck through his heel and into a piece of

157

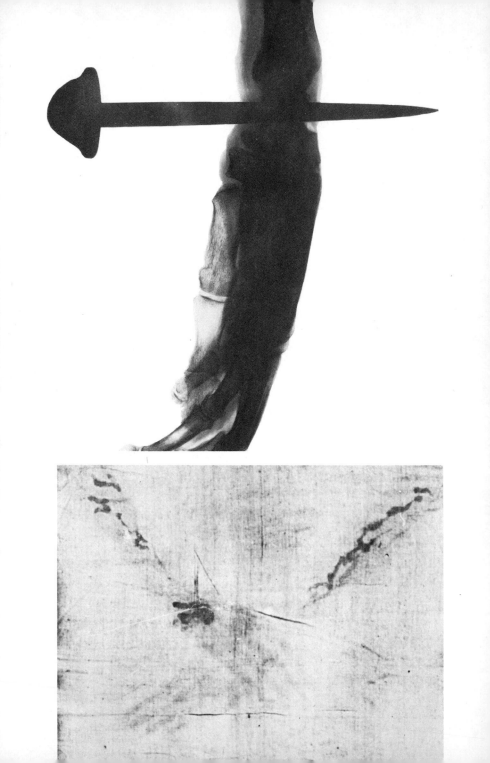

The nailing

8- to 10-inch Roman nails like the one at right were hammered through the hands and feet of the figure in the shroud. (RKW)
In order to support the weight of an adult affixed to a cross, the nails would have had to pass through the wrists in what is called Destot's space, illustrated at the top of the opposite page. (HSG)
This would result in marks corresponding to those on the shroud material, below on the opposite page. (HSG)

wood. His other bones showed that the nails for the arms had probably been placed between the radius and ulna bones, the two bones that make up the forearm.

The Romans reserved crucifixion for outcasts; for runaway slaves such as Spartacus; and for political insurgents, as Jesus appeared to be to some. There were three types of crosses: one shaped like a **T**, one like an **X**, and the one like a dagger with hilt. As in the case of Jesus, crucifixion was usually preceded by flogging.

Sometimes the victims were nailed to the cross; sometimes they were tied; sometimes they had a footrest; sometimes, a small seat.

"The Romans invented an almost endless variation in the techniques of crucifixion," wrote Daniel P. Mannix in *The History of Torture.* "Sometimes the victim was nailed by one arm and one leg on an L-shaped pole, sometimes he was crucified head downward—like tradition says St. Peter was. Nero soaked Christians with tar before having them crucified and used them as human torches around his garden at night." ■

Msgr. Giulio Ricci, when I interviewed him in Turin, gave me his own theory about the crucifixion of Jesus, which he had developed from his lifelong study of the marks on the shroud.

"His hands were tied to the crossbeam, shoulder-high, and thus he couldn't have protected himself when he stumbled. Whenever he fell, he would have landed on his face, Judging from some of the contusions on it, it appears he tried to turn his face to avoid the bruises, but he wasn't able to do it very well. The beam must have been in the way. I think eventually he would have died from concussion if the soldiers hadn't stopped it and made Simon of Cyrene carry the cross. They didn't do this out of compassion for Jesus but because they didn't want him to die on the way to Golgotha. His death was a political matter. It was important that he die as an outlaw. And so the soldiers charged with carrying out the crucifixion didn't want to be held responsible if he didn't die that way."

How long does death by crucifixion take? According to Dr. Hermann Moedder, a German radiologist who got university students to volunteer for a test in which they were tied to a cross, the victim would lose consciousness in no more than twelve minutes. An American sindonologist, Rev. Peter Weyland, S.V.D., has lasted longer lashed to a cross. He told his story in *A Sculptor Interprets the Holy Shroud of Turin,* which was published in 1954.

"I set up a large cross and placed a large refinished mirror on the wall in front of it. Thus equipped, I experimented with hanging on the cross from 700 to 800 times for short intervals to observe how a body, fastened with hands and feet and without the use of a footrest or a seat, would hang."

Weyland had first read of the shroud in a 1934 book by Msgr. Arthur S. Barnes, an Oxford University chaplain and a former editor of the *Dublin Review.* In the book Barnes maintained that Jesus' body was wrapped in the shroud on Golgotha and that the images had been transferred to the shroud cloth as the body was carried to the tomb. After reading the book, Weyland began giving lantern slide lectures about the shroud and learning the mechanics of hanging. In 1937 Father Wuenschel asked him to model a crucifix, using the shroud data as a basis for his measurements. He accepted willingly and plunged into the task.

"I decided to make plaster casts of portions of the body while hanging. Thirty-one suspensions, lasting from twenty to twenty-five minutes each, were needed to round out two complete sets of casts covering the whole body."

These casts and the photographs Weyland took during the shorter suspensions served as models for the crucifixes he fashioned. ■

When I approached Dr. Edith Quimby, a radiologist at Columbia University Medical School, she willingly agreed to give me whatever help she could, as did Professor Carpenter; Dr. Quimby had been recommended to me by the Miami radiologist, Harold Davis.

Over **In the 1930s Rev. Peter Weyland, S.V.D., experimented with the mechanics of crucifixion before fashioning a crucifix based on the data in the shroud.** (HSG)

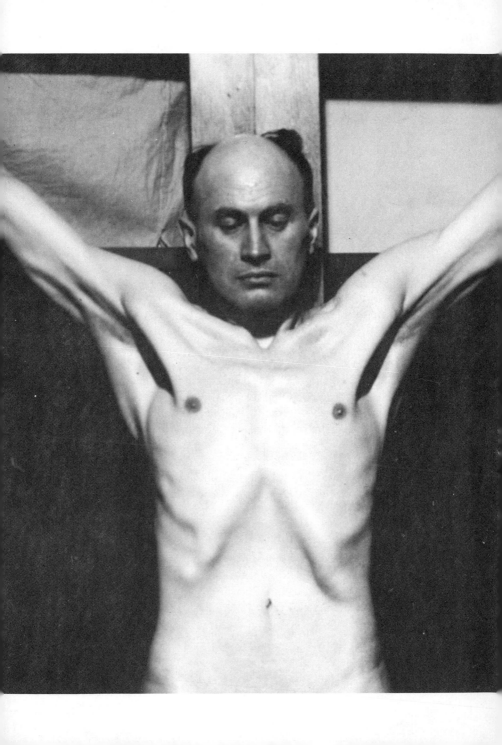

After hearing the shroud story and examining the photographs, she said she didn't have the slightest idea how the images could have been formed.

When I broached the possibility that the images looked as though they might have been produced by scorching, she suggested I see Dr. Ernest Wood, a radiologist at the Neurological Institute of New York; he was an expert in thermography, the use of bodily heat in diagnostic medicine. Dr. Quimby called him and made an appointment for me.

Thermography, explained Dr. Ernest Wood, grew out of infrared photography which was developed in World War II; today it is used mainly in the detection of breast cancer. The principle behind it is a simple one: heat emanating from the body is used to make diagnostic pictures, and the pictures are negatives.

But there were significant differences, Dr. Wood pointed out, between thermographic pictures and the "pictures" on the shroud. For one thing, it took sophisticated machines to magnify body heat to the extent that a picture could be registered: the magnification was on the order of one million times. For another, the thermographic picture was registered on Polaroid film, not cloth.

The negative was not exactly the same either. The reason the film showed a negative image was that the prominences of the body—nose, cheeks, forehead—were closer to the camera and consequently reflected more heat than recesses like the eye socket. Since heat is what showed up on the film, the prominences would be dark as in a photographic negative. If, however, something were wrong in one of the recesses—for example, if there were an eye infection—that recess would give off more heat and show darker on the film than even the prominences; thus the resulting pictures would not be true negatives.

I couldn't blame George Suski for being angry. He had invested hundreds of thousands of dollars making a color film about the shroud story, and he didn't have a color shot of the shroud in it; it seems no one told him about the 1973 exposition.

Talking with him at the offices of Suski Productions, I learned that he had taken a film crew to England and Italy and had interviewed several sindonologists, the most prominent of whom was Giovanni Judica-Cordiglia. Needless to say, the film did not catch

164

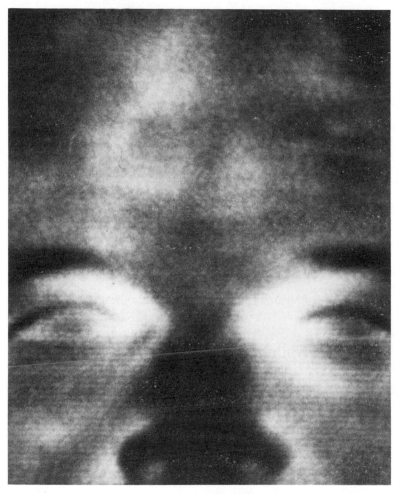

According to the new science of thermography, heat radiating from a human face, magnified one million times, can make an image on Polaroid film like the one above. (EW)

the tremendous depth of the shroud story. The result was a sort of educational film one associates with high school auditoriums.

"By the way," he said to me as I was leaving his office, "you don't know when the next exposition will be, do you?"

Also angry was Thomas Humber, a free-lance writer and editor who was preparing a manuscript on the shroud. Months before the television exposition of the shroud in November 1973, he requested permission to be present, along with other members of the press, with the scholars, clergy, and scientists.

"I volunteered to obey any strictures that might be placed on my presence. I wanted, indeed I needed, to see the mysterious ancient cloth that had for so long occupied my thoughts. In spite of the efforts of Father Rinaldi, who made every effort on my behalf, I was told that no outsiders would be allowed access to the shroud, that there would be no press conference, and that no one would be admitted to the cathedral when the cloth was displayed other than the television crew and Turin officials."

In *The Fifth Gospel: The Miracle of the Holy Shroud,* which was published by Pocket Books in 1974, he went on to say, "I was thus faced with an expensive and frustrating journey, only to sit in a hotel room and see the shroud on Italian television. I decided not to go." ■

New Rochelle

THE LAST EXPERT on my list was Len Barcus, an astronomer, inventor, and optical physicist. He had been recommended to me by Dr. Karlis Osis, head of the American Society of Psychical Research, for whom he had developed some testing gadgetry.

Barcus met me at the train station in New Rochelle and during the short drive from the station to his house he filled me in on his background. With degrees in mathematics and astronomy from the University of Virginia, he taught at Columbia University. After World War II he developed optical instrumentation for viewing stars in daylight from high-flying aircraft.

Sitting at the dining-room table in his home, I told the shroud story for what seemed the thousandth time and showed him the shroud photographs. Simple contact, that's how the images were made, he said; simple contact with a corpse. When I told him how Vignon's and Judica-Cordigila's contact experiments had failed to reproduce sharp images, Barcus persisted. He dropped a handkerchief over a bust on a pedestal; then he realized that although the basic features would come out, the subtleties, the curves, the depressions which would give the image a lifelike quality would not. "Yes, it is puzzling, isn't it?" he said, backing away from the bust.

The scorch theory interested him next. I was about to present the first objection to the scorch theory—the cloth wasn't damaged —when he said that a singe burn was simple oxidation. When a hot iron momentarily touches a sheet, the singe, or scorch, that results causes oxidation or browning to occur. The same thing happens, he went on to explain, when shrimp are dropped into boiling water; the only visible change is that the shrimp turn a darker shade of pink.

Perhaps, I mused later, the images on the shroud had not been scorched onto the linen; they were cooked on.

In the spring of 1976, the reports from those who had participated in the 1969 secret study were released. They were inconclusive. The experts said no evidence that the shroud was a fake had been found, but their tests had only been preliminary and no concrete statement on authenticity could be released.

Soon after that declaration, however, it became known that one participant had not sent in his findings with the others. This was Prof. Max Frei, the criminologist from Zurich, Switzerland. According to Father Rinaldi, who printed a synopsis of the study's findings and mailed it to shroud enthusiasts, Frei's late report said: "I can state with certainty that the Turin shroud dates from the time of Christ."

Rinaldi explained: "Scrapings from the shroud, which [Frei] analyzed, revealed the presence on the Turin cloth of certain pollen fossils that 'could only have originated from plants that grew exclusively in Palestine at the time of Christ.' Frei said

167

his pollen studies bear out the traditional history of the shroud's itinerary. He found pollen fossils from Turkey (Constantinople) dating back to the time of the Crusades, and others from France in the Middle Ages."

In addition, the reports, while not ruling out the possibility that the cloth contained particles of ancient blood matter, said that preliminary results from the testing of several threads indicated there was no blood. Vignon's idea that the stains are possibly "photographs" of blood clots, such as a flash of heat or light might make, thus gained more credibility—at least temporarily.

Simultaneously, two officer scientists at the Air Force Academy had become interested in the shroud. Using computers to analyze data from the Enrie photos, they had verified Vignon's idea that the image was uniformly lighter and darker in proportion to the distance between the body and the cloth. So uniform, in fact, was the variation, Captains John Jackson and Eric Jumper told the January 15, 1977 *Catholic Register* that there was no question in their minds that images had been produced by some "physical process"—apparently other than human artistry—and they tended to favor a "thermogram," an image formed by heat.

In contrast to Barbet, the two felt that, with the aid of computer-enhanced photos of the shroud, they had discovered thumbs on the hands folded over the loins and possibly two ancient coins resting on the eyes.

"Such a thing was part of the Jewish burial custom," says the *Register* story, and the two said they now plan to "try to identify the coins, to see if we can date them."

Sindonology had indeed moved into the Space Age. ∎

Miami

BACK in Miami, having interviewed as many sindonologists and shroud enthusiasts as I could find, and having consulted as many experts in the sciences touching upon the shroud, I could now contemplate the two major problems—the authenticity of the shroud and the origin of the images on the shroud—and draw

conclusions I never could have dreamed of twelve months ago.

First, the cloth is unique. Nowhere in my wanderings did I come across a burial cloth, or the record of a burial cloth, with body imprints.

Second, the imprinted cloth is old, at least six hundred years old as the "shroud of Turin," probably two thousand years old as the "Image of Edessa."

Third, the linen of the cloth and the herringbone twill could have been manufactured and distributed throughout the Mediterranean world at least two thousand years ago.

Fourth, the imprints on the cloth are those of a human corpse, at least according to the testimony of several dozen pathologists.

Fifth, the imprints on the cloth show that the man was scourged with a *flagrum,* lacerated around the head, forced to carry the crossbeam on his shoulders, and nailed through the hands and feet; they show also that after the man expired, his body was wounded in the side.

Sixth, the sufferings and death as recorded on the shroud correspond to the sufferings and death described in the Gospels.

Seventh, before one is tempted to think that the man in the shroud is Jesus Christ, he should consider the possibility of forgery.

The forger would have had to acquire a body more alive than dead, then mutilate it according to the quite specific details in the Gospels.

Then the forger would have had to transfer the image of the dead man onto the cloth by one of two possible ways. Either he would have had to press a cloth onto the front and back of the body and thereby produce an image as sharp as the shroud's—something Vignon and Judica-Cordiglia were unable to do. Or he would have had to use the corpse as a model and paint the image onto the cloth. But no pigment has ever been found on the cloth by those who took the trouble to look.

The forger working in France or thereabouts around or before 1350 would have to have been either an overzealous monk whose piety got the better of him or an arrogant swindler who wanted to make a bundle in the underground relic market. Both of these possibilities strike me as unlikely, since the portrayal of Jesus on

170

the shroud is nontraditional, non-European; details like the cap or miter of thorns, the nails through the wrists instead of through the palms, and the nakedness of the loins would not inspire the devotional or artistic sensibilities of fourteenth-century Europe; rather they would have gotten the forger burned at the stake. Moreover, the accuracy of details like these would not be common knowledge to a potential forger for centuries to come.

Eighth, before one rushes to embrace the man in the shroud as Jesus Christ, he should consider the statistical probability against the anonymous victim's having suffered, died, and been buried in exactly the same way as Jesus. The odds against this having happened, according to Paul de Gail, a French Jesuit priest and engineer, are 225 billion to one. Italian physicist Tino Zeuli, who quoted de Gail in the April 1974 issue of *Sindon,* went on to liken the possibility to a brick in the street suddenly sprouting wings and taking off.

Ninth, all things considered, therefore, it is not unreasonable to conclude that the man in the shroud is indeed the man we call Jesus Christ.

Tenth, that Jesus is the man in the shroud does not in and of itself prove or disprove that Jesus came back to life, rose from the dead.

To get some appreciation of what is held as theological fact by many, one must reconstruct what happened during those thirty-six hours or so after death.

The tomb, a rocky chamber carved out of a hillside, a stone rolled against the door, is dark and silent. Lying on a slab is a long, rectangular cocoon, the hills and valleys clearly being the contours of a human body. Jesus lay there, face up, a ribbon around the head and chin to keep the mouth closed, bags of spices packed along the sides of his dead body.

At some unknown moment in the dead of night, the air in the tomb becomes electric.

Minute vibrations at first, the sort that could be detected by sensitive twentieth-century instruments; then they dramatically increase until they shake the ground and blow the boulder from the door.

A glow, faint at first, emanating from the shroud suddenly in-

tensifies until rays of light shoot through the threads, star-filled golden rays filling the tomb and pouring out the door.

For thirty seconds—no more—the blinding, pulsating movement continues.

The source of the activity is the corpse, the body, somehow being revitalized, dematerialized, its mass being converted into energy, pure energy, which in the material world is radiant white light.

The body rises from the slab through the cloth, hovers for a moment in midair, then disappears.

The cocoon collapses. Darkness returns. Shouts of "Earthquake! Earthquake!" diminish as the two guards run for their lives. And in the air, the distinct odor of scorched linen.

When dawn comes, the women in Jesus' life draw tentatively toward the tomb, look in the opening, and see the shroud unopened, still wrapped, but definitely deflated. The body is gone. At sunrise the disciples come. John enters the tomb, puts his hand on the cloth, and presses it to the slab. Jesus is there no longer. The disciples and the women quickly gather up the burial garments—the chin band is still inside the shroud—and the spice bags and leave before the Romans can return.

At another time, in another place, when they have a chance to gather their wits, they will discover the figure of their master imprinted on the inside of the shroud. The images would be faint, probably not as dark as the passage of time and exposure to air have made them; and the images would be negative ones, a phenomenon that would also become clearer with the passage of time. They would pay more attention to the images on the shroud, the disciples would, if they weren't already waiting, with the greatest anticipation, for Jesus himself, who, before his death, had promised to visit them after he rose from the dead.

Bibliography

Abbott, Walter. "Did Christ Leave a Picture of Himself on the Shroud of Turin?" *The Pilot* (Boston), April 17, 1954.

————. "Shroud, The Holy." *Catholic Encyclopedia,* Supplement II, Seventh Section, vol. XVII, 1957.

————. "The Shroud and the Holy Face." *American Ecclesiastical Review,* vol. CXXXII, 1955.

Adams, Frank O. *A Scientific Search for the Face of Jesus.* Tucson, Ariz.: Psychical Aid Foundation, 1972.

Allen-Griffiths, D. *Whose Image and Likeness?* Nottingham: The J. & M. Publishing Co., 1964.

Barbet, Pierre. *Doctor at Calvary.* New York: P. J. Kenedy & Sons, 1953; New York: Image Books, 1963.

Barclay, Vera. *Face of a King.* Bognor Regis, England: Century Arts Press, 1954.

————. "Holy Shroud—Guidance of Dead Sea Skeletons." *Catholic Herald* (London), March 18, 1960.

————. "On the First Reactions to the Photographs of the Holy Shroud." *The Altar Server,* June 1959.

Barnes, Arthur S. *The Holy Shroud of Turin.* London: Burns, Oates and Washbourne, 1934.

————. "The New Evidence Concerning the Holy Shroud of Turin." *Dublin Review,* vol. CXCII, 1933.

Beecher, P. A. *The Holy Shroud: A Reply to the Rev. Herbert Thurston, S.J.* Dublin: M. H. Gill and Son, Ltd., 1928.

————. "The Crucifixion as Told in the Holy Shroud," *Irish Ecclesiastical Record,* LV (1940).

Boyles, Andrew. *No Passing Glory.* London: Collins, 1955.

Bucklin, Robert. "The Medical Aspects of the Crucifixion of Our Lord Jesus Christ." *Linacre Quarterly,* February 1958.

————. "The Legal and Medical Aspects of the Trial and Death of Christ." *Medicine, Science, and the Law,* January 1970.

Bulst, Werner. *The Shroud of Turin.* Milwaukee: Bruce Publishing Co., 1957.

Caylor, Ron. "Jeane Dixon Exclusive." *National Enquirer,* June 30, 1974.

Chalice, The. Summer 1937 issue of the magazine. Brooklyn: Monastery of the Precious Blood, 1937.

Cheshire, Leonard. *The Face of Victory.* London: Hutchinson, 1961.

————. "I Saw the Face of Christ." London *Daily Sketch,* March 7, 1955.

————. *Pilgrimage to the Shroud.* New York: McGraw-Hill Book Company, 1956.

————. "How Christ Was Crucified." London *Picture Post,* April 9, 1955.

Doepner, Herman. *The Turin Shroud Speaks.* Unpublished manuscript in the collection of Richard Orareo.

Devan, Donald; Jumper, Eric; Jackson, John. "A Scientific Search for New Images on the Holy Shroud of Turin by Computer Enhancement." Unpublished manuscript.

Furlong, Francis P. "Jesus Christ Who Was Crucified." Linacre Quarterly, vol. 19, 1952.

Green, Maurus. "Enshrouded in Silence." *Ampleforth Journal,* vol. LXXIV, 1969.

Humber, Thomas. *The Fifth Gospel: The Miracle of the Holy Shroud.* New York: Pocket Books, 1974.

Hynek. R. W. *Science and the Holy Shroud.* Chicago: Benedictine Press, 1936.

————. *The True Likeness.* New York: Sheed & Ward, 1951.

Johnson, Kendall. *The Living Aura.* New York, Hawthorn Books, 1975.

Katz, Robert. *The Fall of the House of Savoy.* New York: Macmillan Publishing Co., Inc., 1971.

Kilner, J. W. *The Aura.* New York: Samuel Weiser, 1973.

Krippner, S. and Rubin, D. *The Kirlian Aura.* New York: Doubleday, 1974.

Mackey, H. B. "The Holy Shroud of Turin." *Dublin Review,* vol. CXXII, 1903.

Mannix, Daniel P. *The History of Torture.* New York: Dell, 1964.

Meyer, Karl E. "Were You There When They Photographed My Lord?" *Esquire,* August 1971.

Naber, Hans. *See* Reban, John.

O'Gorman, P. W. "The Holy Shroud of Jesus Christ: New Discovery of the Cause of the Impression." *The American Ecclesiastical Review,* vol. CII, 1940.

————. "The Holy Shroud of Christ: Reply to Arguments Against its Authenticity," *The Irish Catholic,* December 18 and 25, 1941; January 1, 1942.

O'Rahilly, Alfred. Unpublished manuscript. Esopus, N.Y.: Wuenschel Collection.

————. "Jewish Burial," *Irish Ecclesiastical Record,* LVIII (1940).

————. "The Burial of Christ," *Irish Ecclesiastical Record,* LVIII (1940) and LIX (1941).

Ostrander, Sheila, and Schroeder, Lynn. *Psychic Discoveries Behind the Iron Curtain.*

Otterbein, Adam. "Shroud, Holy," *The New Catholic Encyclopedia,* New York, 1967.

Proszymski, Kazimir de. *The Authentic Photograph of Christ.* London: Search Publishing Co., 1932.

Reban, John (Naber, Hans). *Inquest on Jesus Christ—Did He Die on the Cross?* London: Leslie Frewin, 1967.

Rinaldi, Peter M. "The Holy Shroud." *Sign,* vol. XIII, 1934.

————. *I Saw the Holy Shroud.* Tampa, Florida: Don Bosco Messenger, 1938.

————. "I Saw the Holy Shroud." *Sign,* vol. LIII, February 1974.

————. *It Is the Lord.* New York: Vantage Press, 1972; New York: Warner Paperback Library, 1973.

Sandhurst, B. G. *The Silent Witness.* Unpublished manuscript from the collection of Rev. Maurus Green, O.S.B.

Sava, Anthony. "The Blood and Water from the Side of Christ," *The American Ecclesiastical Review,* vol. CXXXVIII, 1958.

————. "The Wound in the Side of Christ." *Catholic Biblical Quarterly,* vol. XVI, 1957.

Schonfield, Hugh. Preface to Kazimir de Proszymski's *The Authentic Photograph of Christ.* London: Search Publishing Co., 1932.

Sullivan, Barbara M. "How in Fact Was Jesus Laid in the Tomb?" *National Review,* July 20, 1973.

175

Thurston, Herbert. "The Holy Shroud as a Scientific Problem." *The Month,* vol. CI, 1903.

———. "The Problem of the Holy Shroud," *The Irish Ecclesiastical Record,* vol. XXIV, 1919.

Vignon, Paul. *The Shroud of Christ.* New Hyde Park, N.Y.: University Books, 1970.

——— and Wuenschel, Edward. "The Problem of the Holy Shroud." *Scientific American,* vol. XCIII, 1937.

Walsh, John. *The Shroud.* New York: Random House, 1963.

Weatherhead, Leslie D. *The Manner of the Resurrection.* Nashville, Tenn.: Abingdon Press, 1959.

Weyland, Peter. *A Sculptor Interprets the Holy Shroud of Turin.* Esopus, N.Y.: The Holy Shroud Guild, 1954.

Willis, David. "Did He Die on the Cross?" *Ampleforth Journal,* vol. LXXIV, 1969.

———. "False Prophet and the Holy Shroud," *The Tablet,* June 13, 1970.

Wilson, Ian. "A Gift to Our Proof-demanding Era?" *Catholic Herald* (London), November 16, 1973.

Wuenschel, Edward A. "The Holy Shroud of Turin." *Perpetual Help,* vol. XIII, 1956. This article also appeared, in condensed form, in *Catholic Digest,* vol. XIV, 1950.

———. "The Holy Shroud of Turin: Eloquent Record of the Passion." *American Ecclesiastical Review,* vol. XCIII, 1935.

———. "The Holy Shroud: Present State of the Question." *American Ecclesiastical Review,* vol. CII, 1940.

———. "The Photograph of Christ," *Pax,* XV (1937).

———. "The Holy Shroud and Art," *Liturgical Arts,* IX (1941).

———. *Self-portrait of Christ: The Holy Shroud of Turin.* Esopus, N.Y.: The Holy Shroud Guild, 1954.

———. "The Shroud of Turin and the Burial of Christ." *The Catholic Biblical Quarterly:* vol. VII, 1945; vol. VIII, 1946.

———. "The Truth About the Holy Shroud." *American Ecclesiastical Review,* vol. CXXIX, 1953.

Index

177

178

Robe-of-Christ theory, 47
Robert, Spigo, 41
Robert de Clari, 97
Rocher-Jauneau, Madelaine, 67
Romanese, Prof., 16
Romanus Lecapenus, 93
Rush, Dr. John, 118, 152

Savio, Msgr. Pietro, 35, 53
Schonfield, Hugh, 78
Schroeder, Lynn, 141, 142
Scorch theory, 123, *124*, *125*, 126,
144, 152, 164, 167
Scotti, Msgr. Pietro, 22, 110
Scourging. *See* Flagellation marks
Shroud of Turin
Byzantine history (to 1204), 84–98
carbon 14 dating and, 17, 35, 144–
45, 148
cause of death theories, 70–71,
72–73, 74–81
conclusions, summary, 169–71, 173
contact stain theory, 16, 62, *63*, 64,
70, 167
descriptions, physiology, race, 3–4,
30, *32*, 41–42, 45, 116–17,
129–31, 136
exhibitions (1898, 1931, 1933), 1,
5, 8, 10, 11, 13, 14, 17–18, 30,
45
flash-of-heat-and-light theory, 126,
168
iconography theory, 84–98, *87–91*,
131
illustrations of, *6*, *7*, *29*, *32*, *38*, *39*,
40, *50*, *51*, *55*, *58*, *87*, *158*, *172*
illustrations of reproductions or
other renderings, *2*, *46*, *59*,
112–13, *132–35*, *174*
Jewish burial practices and, 117–
18, 155–57, 168
Lirey to House of Savoy history
(1354/6–1452), 100, 105
non-death theory, 1, 43–44, 45,
69–81
painting, or dye theory, 57, *58*, *59*,
60, 109
pre-Lirey history (1204–1354/6),
22, 98–100
radiation theories (Kirlian photography, or radiation field pho-

tography), 119–20, 123, 127–
28, 129, 139–43, 144, 145,
146–47, 148–49, 150–52, 164,
165
secret commission study
(1969), 17, 19, 22, 35, 37, 41,
42, 44, 45, 49, 67, 77
scorch theory, 123, *124*, *125*, 126,
144, 152, 164, 167
TV exposition (1973), 1, 26, 30,
34, 35, 37, *40*, 41–42, 48–49,
50, 51
vapograph theory, 16, 65–66, 119,
128, 152
Siegmund, Dr., 74
Sixtus IV, Pope, 49
Spellman, Francis Cardinal, *106*, 107
Stephen III, Pope, 94
Stewart, T. Dale, 129, 130, 131
Suski, George, 164

Templars, 98–100
Thermography theory, 164, *165*. *See
also* Radiation theories
Thurston, Herbert, 109, 110
Tilney, Mrs. I. Sheldon, 111, 115
Tonelli, Fr. Antonio, 10
Trout, E. Dale, 120

Umberto II of Savoy, 11–14, *12*, 27,
114, 115

Vaccari, Alberto, 110
Vala, Leo, 130, 131, 174
Vapograph theory, 16, 65–66, 119,
128, 152
Victor Emmanuel III, 13
Vignon, Paul, 22, 56–57, 60, 62, 64,
65–66, 70, 85, 92, 96, 103, 104,
109, 115, 117, 119, 152, 167,
168, 170
Villandre, Charles, 15
Vitalis, Ordericus, 95, 97
Volckringer, Dr. Jean, 139, 140, 142,
143, 144
Von Campenhausen, Dr., 74

Walsh, John, *114*, 115
Weyland, Rev. Peter, 161, *162–63*
Willis, Dr. David, 72, 75, 76

179

Willis, Thomas, 75
Wilson, Ian, 92, 93–100, 105, 131, 155
Wollam, Josephine, 27–28, *80*, 81, 83
Wood, Dr. Ernest, 164
Wuenschel, Fr. Edward A., 22, 101, *102*, 103–105, 107, 111, 115, 118, 123, 153, 155, 161

Zeuli, Tino, 171
Zlotnic, Dr. Dov., 118, 156–57